Advance Praise for The Secret Lies Within

"Anne Beiler's courage to reveal heart-wrenching secrets along her journey to becoming one of America's best-known business leaders is utterly captivating. Her book shows readers how to bravely rise up and turn the piercing light of truth upon the web of deception that has entrapped them in a prison of silence. To all who read *The Secret Lies Within*, may you discover the keys to the Light and bountiful Godwinks."

~**SQUIRE RUSHNELL**, author, Godwink Book series

"Secrets. That powerful word pulled me in instantly! Finally, someone who has experienced trauma personally is writing about a meaningful and instructional approach to survivors of sexual abuse and family secrets. Anne's guide for those who have been deeply hurt and affected by sexual trauma is a MUST read. I will recommend it to my clients who are trying to find their path through the darkness of abuse."

~**MARK MEANS**, Licensed Marriage and Family Therapist

"*The Secret Lies Within* shows Anne's honesty and bravery, qualities she possesses abundantly. Anne addresses subjects that are as intensely personal and painful as they are redemptive. Her reliance on Jesus lights the way for readers who have experienced trauma as well as those who have walked through trauma with loved ones."

~**BARRY H. COREY**, President of Biola University and author of *Love Kindness: Discover the Power of a Forgotten Christian Virtue*

"At 9 years of age, a drunk driver slid across the divide killing my dad and debilitating my mom for life. As *The Secret Lies Within* effectively unveils, tragedy can become an unwelcome companion for life without discovering the truth and its active ingredients to heal. Read this book and Anne's transparency and insights will offer you a liberating path from living wounded to becoming a wounded healer."

~**DAVE DONALDSON**, Former Committee Member, Substance Abuse Mental Health Service Administration (SAMHSA) C-SAT; Co-founder, Convoy of Hope and CityServe International

"I've known Anne Beiler for many years. She is an intelligent, sensitive, caring person who just loves deeply. Her story of survival is so moving. Her resilience is admirable. I know this story of her life will 'change your life'. We all live with secrets and Anne's story will certainly help us all to deal with our inner pain. I love this woman ... my dear friend. This book is a must read!"

~**LILY ISAAC**, Multi Award Winning Vocalist, Author of *You Don't Cry Out Loud: The Lily Isaacs Story*

"*The Secret Lies Within* is as much a guide for those that have experienced trauma as it is a collection of inspiring stories of overcoming. Anne doesn't shy away from diving into the hard issues like abuse, affairs, depression, and death but she has found a way to do that while leaving you inspired to change your own life. Anyone affected by trauma needs to read this!"

~**SCOTT WILSON**, Oaks Church, Senior Pastor, Author, *Clear the Stage: Making Room for God*

"Anne Beiler has secrets. She knows the secret ingredient in her famous Auntie Anne's Soft Pretzels. She knows the secret to success by creating an international business from one stand at a farmer's market. She also knows secrets can destroy. In *The Secret Lies Within*, Anne will reveal the secret to living a life free from bondage to your past mistakes. Join her on this journey from the darkness to light."

~**JOHN C MAXWELL**, Author and Speaker

"Making yourself vulnerable can be scary. Very scary. But I am convinced that in doing so, that's where real, transformative ministry takes place. This book will be transformative in your life. Anne's transparency shows us we are not the 'only one'. Her honesty and authenticity are refreshing and healing. As you read this book you hold in your hand, you will find a safe friend."

~**RUTH GRAHAM**, author of *In Every Pew Sits A Broken Heart and Fear Not Tomorrow, God Is Already There*

"Auntie Anne is widely recognized as the successful founder of the world's largest hand-rolled soft pretzel franchise company. Few would guess that behind her success is heartbreaking pain, loss, and abuse. In *The Secret Lies Within*, Anne shares her story with vulnerability, leading us from pain to healing and from despair to hope. For anyone who has suffered trauma or felt hopelessness, Anne's story reveals a path out of the darkness that offers healing, redemption, and freedom."

~**PETER GREER**, president and CEO, HOPE International and coauthor Mission Drift

"In finding the courage to tell the story of her long journey to wholeness, Anne Beiler throws a lifeline to others who have been silenced and paralyzed by the shame that follows abuse, especially abuse perpetrated by those who should be the trusted keepers of safe havens. Redemption is not instantaneous, but a process of persistent grasping and holding to the buoy within our reach, the buoy that itself is held by the rope of faith and tied to the strong rock of God's relentless love for us all. Emily Sutherland writes this story with clarity and deep empathy."

~GLORIA GAITHER

The Secret Lies Within

The Secret Lies Within

An Inside Out Look at Overcoming Trauma and Finding Purpose in the Pain

ANNE BEILER
Founder of Auntie Anne's Pretzels

 Emily Sutherland

NEW YORK

LONDON • NASHVILLE • MELBOURNE • VANCOUVER

The Secret Lies Within

An Inside Out Look at Overcoming Trauma and Finding Purpose in the Pain

Published in New York, New York, by Morgan James Publishing. Morgan James is a trademark of Morgan James, LLC. www.MorganJamesPublishing.com

ISBN 9781642793116 paperback
ISBN 9781642793109 case laminate hardcover
ISBN 9781642793123 eBook
ISBN 9781642793130 audio book
Library of Congress Control Number: 2018912155

Cover Design by:
Rachel Lopez
www.r2cdesign.com

Interior Design by:
Christopher Kirk
www.GFSstudio.com

Morgan James is a proud partner of Habitat for Humanity Peninsula and Greater Williamsburg. Partners in building since 2006.

Get involved today! Visit
MorganJamesPublishing.com/giving-back

To all of you who have experienced pain and trauma in your lifetime. You are loved, you are not alone, and you have a story to tell.

To our sweet Angie—your time on earth was short, but your impact has lasted a lifetime. I can't wait to see you again.

To my husband Jonas, my very good man, without whom I wouldn't be here.

Table of Contents

INTRODUCTION

Secrets

Secrets are an invisible burden we were not meant to carry alone.

S ecrets.
When we were young children, secrets came with a rush of excitement. What could be more thrilling than being "in the know" about a surprise, or giving a gift we couldn't wait for the recipient to unwrap? Being trusted with a secret made us feel special back then.

As the years unfolded, however, some of us found ourselves carrying heavier secrets—secrets that could hurt someone or that came with consequences we were unprepared to face. Family secrets, choices we made, pacts with siblings or friends, things that happened to us, or even things we don't remember that nonetheless forever impact us ... those kinds of secrets become more complicated. Their weight presses in, often forcing us to cover secrets with more secrets and eventually pulling us into isolation.

At first, a certain allure might pacify our vulnerable depths, not completely unlike the fun of those innocent secrets. But as those secrets stack up against the framework of our inner life, they begin to block out the light. They crowd out joy and stifle peace. We might develop coping mechanisms that help us survive for a while, but those only last for so long. Slowly, but surely, our secrets convince us we have no other option than to remain stuck in the shadowy darkness.

———•◆•———

I am all too familiar with the smothering darkness that comes with bearing secrets.

I was convinced I could never tell anyone my story. The shame of my secrets convinced me that darkness was what I deserved. That shame took away my hope, stole my voice, and threatened to paralyze me so I could never find my way out. Despair took up residence for many years and the isolation was profound. So profound, in fact, that I started to believe I would be better off dead.

My journey from a simple Amish upbringing to owning an international franchise is not a feel-good, rags-to-riches story. Rather, it is a story about first losing my way and then deciding not to settle for darkness. It is a story that, honestly, will be difficult to read at times.

It was difficult to write, too.

It's not the story I *wanted* …
but it's the story I *have*.

Among the many lies I believed, I thought *if only* I could change my circumstances, I would be happier. *If only* I had a different husband ... *If only* my daughter hadn't died ... *If only* my kids were more compliant ... *If only* I could get far enough away from the memories of abuse and failures ... maybe *then* I could finally be happy.

It took a very long time to discover that brokenness and isolation would continue to follow me while I still held my secrets close.

My story reveals the secrets I carried and the emotions I buried. You will witness the power those secrets held over me and the ripple effect on the people I love.

I share my story as it *was*, not as I *wish it was*.

Eventually, mine became a story of healing and redemption. If my life has taught me anything, it's taught me that people all around us are living in pain ... and have no idea how they will survive. Mothers, Fathers, Children—God-fearing people. Yes, even us sincere, God-fearing people can lose our way.

I know now that there is nothing spiritual about silence. Silence only serves to bring a slow death to the state of being fully alive. Therefore, I invite you into the most painful experiences of my life for one simple reason: to hold up a light. I want to bring you with me on a journey toward healing and freedom.

**I found my voice, and eventually my freedom,
one moment at a time.**

I don't want to waste a single moment of my pain. And my passage from despair to freedom in no way meant my life became pain-free. Sometimes healing feels like ripping off a scab and then pouring salt water into the wound. Sometimes a memory is triggered without warning and takes me back 40 years to painful moments that altered my life forever. Even decades later, there are times when pain utterly flattens me.

I used to blame God for my pain. I was taught from a young age that God was a present help in times of trouble, but I did not see, or feel, or even believe He was present in my life at times.

Now, I can look back and see He was there the whole time. His intervention came at critical times, even when I didn't know He was close. I picture an avid swimmer out in the ocean, far from shore, who feels as if her training should be enough to keep moving toward the shore. Her arms get weak because the swim is difficult. She feels tired of fighting against the forces of nature. But then she recalls the words her coach has spoken time, after time, after time. He believed she could make it to the shore, even when she didn't. My pain was that ocean and God was that coach. When I was sure I didn't have what it took to move another inch, strength would come that I didn't know I had. His Presence, though invisible, was no less present in my pain. What I knew in my head as a child, I now know in my heart from personal experience. He was always there.

That pain I once tried to pray away or numb I am now able to sit with and experience. I have learned to manage the emotion in a way that takes me forward instead of backward, thanks to the help of wise counselors, psychiatric professionals, trustworthy friends, and a husband who loves me unconditionally.

I did not get to decide how my story began, but I *do* get to choose how it ends. And, so do you, even if that's hard to believe right now.

I share my story as authentically as I know how, and I have asked a few courageous people for permission to share portions of their stories as well. Through our stories, I hope to offer a spark of hope to anyone who feels isolated and stuck in a story they didn't ask for and didn't want.

There *is* a path out of the deepest dark. If I could find it, anyone can.

CHAPTER 1

The Set-Up

"A lot of things you see as a
child remain with you ...
you spend a lot of your life trying to
recapture the experience."
Tim Burton

There is not one kind of person who gets stuck in the dark. It can happen to anyone, anywhere, anytime. From prestigious positions of power to the gutters of desperation, people from every walk of life can find themselves smothered in pain, guilt, blame, and shame, with no light to be found. Even in churches.

Actually, *especially* in churches.

You may be wondering how someone raised in a tight-knit Amish community, the third of eight siblings, could feel isolated. Or you may quietly be wondering why my faith didn't—and couldn't—save me from secrets and shame.

The truth is, I had those same questions when I found myself lost and desperate.

But it didn't happen overnight.

My parents, Amanda and Eli, taught my siblings and I to work hard and never complain. Self-control and productivity are highly valued in the Amish community, and there is a lot of good that comes from those values with working hard as the norm. However, processing our emotions had no place in that culture. There was no space for us to talk about—or even acknowledge—our negative emotions like fear, anger, or disappointment.

When I was three years old, my parents left the Old Order Amish community for a progressive, "Black Car Amish" (also known as Amish Mennonite) community. Anyone who chooses to leave the Old Order Amish is shunned by all Old Order family members for a period of time. My mom grieved cutting ties with her family, yet she never spoke of that grief. There was an underlying sadness in her that we could feel but could never talk about. Looking back now, I'm sure having eight children to care for must have left her feeling overwhelmed on top of her sadness—and she kept it all inside.

My family lived on a farm in Lancaster County, Pennsylvania, and every day except Sunday was spent gardening, cleaning, baking, sewing, milking cows, caring for the animals, mowing, and washing. The outdoor farm tasks were physically difficult for me because I had severe allergies, so my parents allowed me to do my chores indoors to keep my hay fever from flaring up, and I worked in the kitchen next to my mom. I loved being in the kitchen and my mom was very patient with me as I learned. We would often sing hymns together while we baked and prepared meals. I think back on that now and realize just how much power music has to soothe our souls. I know those hymns helped ease the burdens my mom wouldn't verbalize.

Spending so many hours at her side in the kitchen gave me occasional glimpses of the lingering sadness she felt over the loss of her family. Her stifled grief silently modeled how to ignore feelings, lock away pain, and continue working. When I did catch those glimpses of her pain, I tried to ease her burden by working hard and making myself useful. I knew that made her happy.

Not too many years after our transition out of the Old Order Amish community, my parents experienced devastating financial setbacks, which included the loss of our livestock in a lightning storm and an epidemic that killed our entire herd of pigs. This crisis, too, was not discussed openly. There was no family meeting to help us kids understand what was happening or what this financial crisis meant for our family. There were only whispers behind closed doors late at night, whispers quietly communicating that our uncertainty and fear were things we shouldn't talk about.

Another seed planted.

Our dad suffered from severe depression during that time of financial struggle. We had no idea what depression was back then. We just knew something was wrong. He would disappear for periods of time and mom didn't know where he was. If any of us were worried about where he was or if he was going to be okay, we didn't ask. We only asked, "Where's daddy?"

He had been a lively, playful presence in our home until that time, often getting down on the floor to play with us. But depression changed him. The lighthearted, playful side of him we enjoyed in previous years was quietly overshadowed by a dark cloud that would take years to lift.

At the age of 11, I stepped in to help fix this family crisis. I concluded that my parents needed me to be extra responsible—to help them bear the weight of supporting our family—so I worked even harder, pushed through my suppressed worry, and never complained so they knew they could count on me. They began selling handmade goods at a market stand in Philadelphia on the weekends for extra income and it was my job to prepare all the pies and cakes they would need to sell. At that young age, I would bake up to 60 pies and cakes at a time by myself. (To give you an idea of what 60 cakes and pies looks like, imagine a line of them as long as a bowling lane and you're getting pretty close). My mom would leave a list of what needed to be made and I would make sure they were baked to perfection and ready for the market.

In the Amish culture, girls stop attending school after the eighth grade and are expected to work and take on greater responsibility at home. The future of an Amish girl is to become a wife and mom who can cook, clean, sew, garden, raise children, and do her part to support the family. So, in that culture, it was not unusual for someone my age to assume the responsibility of baking for the market.

Despite the normality of my duty, I remember shedding silent tears as I worked alone. I missed my mom's presence during those long hours. I saw my siblings doing their chores outside together while I baked inside and wished I could join them. We had a large baking area in our basement, lit by a single lightbulb hung from the ceiling. The steps leading down were rickety and the floor was a cement slab. There was one table, some mixing bowls, a small electric mixer, and a large pizza oven where I could bake all the pies and cakes at once. My dad built long cement shelves lining the walls where we stored canned goods and I cooled the pies on those shelves. There, in the basement kitchen, I felt excluded from the carefree days of childhood. But expressing those feelings was not an option. Asking for help never crossed my mind. I learned to push down my feelings of loneliness because my parents had trusted me with a task and I wanted to show them how well I could do it. Knowing they were pleased was all I wanted.

If there is any Amish value stronger than hard work, it is humility. Children are seldom praised for their work because too much praise might make them proud. I didn't expect to hear my parents say, "Anne, thank you for doing a great job on these pies. Your hard work is so helpful to our family." Although I knew that's how they felt in other ways. My mom's term of endearment for me was to call me "Anna Betz" and when she called me that, I knew she was pleased. She would occasionally tell me, "Dengy feh des do," which was Pennsylvania Dutch for "thank you for doing this." I also overheard my dad at the farmer's market telling customers that I made all the pies. I could tell by the tone of his voice that he was pleased with me, and that was all I needed.

There were no televisions, radios, or other electronic devices to distract us from having meaningful conversations, yet our family's communication never included our fears, questions, or frustrations. The Amish lifestyle is steeped in principled living, discipline, and faith. What we didn't understand was the way God designed our bodies, hearts, and minds—that He created emotions for our benefit. I never imagined that negative emotions like anger, fear, and hurt are a God-given warning system, a release valve of sorts to get our attention when we encounter something we need to express, process, and reconcile.

Reinforcing this thought process were sayings I grew up hearing, like this one:

Little children love each other,
Do not give each other pain.
When one speaks to you in anger
Do not answer them again.

According to that message, if someone treats us badly, we should not confront them or hold them accountable. We were taught to look the other way. Whenever we were hurt by someone else, we knew the script: "Obey, don't complain, and don't talk about it." Another common phrase we heard was: "Today is a good day to stop grumbling."

In spite of all the wonderful, innocent experiences of my childhood, so many of those ultimately toxic messages took root in my heart. I don't blame anyone for the beliefs I internalized during those formative years. However, it was essential for me to understand how those mindsets played out in ways that nearly destroyed me later in life.

Like any child, I was unaware of the beliefs I was adopting about myself and my role in our family. Without awareness, I stepped into my role as I understood it: work hard, never complain, and make sure everyone is provided for. I wanted my family to know they could depend on me and we lived by the unspoken rules of not talking openly about things we didn't understand and not expressing negative feelings. Those rules were exemplified by my mother on a daily basis. Families who live by these rules hurt each other, then ignore the pain. I didn't realize I was internalizing those messages, nor did I have any idea how much they would impact my own family years down the road.

———◆◦◆◦◆———

Science tells us that pain refuses to be ignored. The body and mind know, even if we never acknowledge our own pain. Pain makes an indelible imprint on our brains and can have long-lasting physical ramifications. We get high blood pressure, heart disease, diabetes, and more. Stress and anxiety disorders are becoming an epidemic in our society. Unhealed pain plays out in our bodies in countless ways.

Fear. Hurt. Anger. Disappointment. Abandonment. Even if we had those feelings only as little children and rationalized them as adults, they never go away quietly.

Some of us learn to keep a tight lid on our emotions, turning inward until we find ourselves deeply depressed and anxious. (Looking back, my father's depression made perfect sense when I realized that he had been taught the same rules by his parents.) Others fall into a pattern of bottling up pain as long as possible, eventually exploding over something seemingly small, releasing long-ignored emotions that needed a way out. Many of us also learn to numb our pain. We look for temporary relief through food, alcohol, drugs, shopping, self-harm, gambling, adrenaline, sex, work … the list goes on and on. Those momentary escapes can become addictive and sabotage our lives, creating more pain rather than less, and so the vicious cycle goes.

What we learn from our family while we're young provides a foundation that we continue to build on for the rest of our lives. Every family has patterns that they oftentimes unknowingly establish. We learn them as a child and it becomes the way our own family operates. As adults, we carry those patterns into our relationships with others. They influence our behaviors and mindset on a daily basis.

At some point, however, any unhealthy mindsets we have learned stop serving us in the way they once did. Ignoring or numbing pain also numbs the feelings we *want* to feel, like joy, satisfaction, and connection. And those "weak" or "unspiritual" emotions we would rather ignore don't go away on their own. When allowed to fester, they cause far-reaching damage both to us and the people we care about.

The inability to process experiences authentically is not unique to Amish families. I have friends from all walks of life describe a wide range of circumstances that set them up for a life of secrets. My sister's husband, Mike, poignantly describes memories of his father's violent alcoholic rages and his mother's silence as "… an atmosphere of hopelessness." When parents are not dealing with their own feelings of pain, anger, or sadness, those feelings do not go away. Rather, they are passed along unintentionally through words or silent attitudes they clearly communicate to their children. Children unknowingly respond to that pain by believing silent messages such as: "Telling the truth is not a good idea" or "There are certain things I can't trust anyone to know about me" and even "My feelings don't matter, so it's safer not to feel anything."

**The three rules of every
toxic relationship are:
don't talk, don't trust, don't feel.**

I was stuck in that toxic cycle long before I ever could recognize that pattern. Those toxic beliefs are the bedrock of isolation and disconnection and offer the perfect set-up for a life of secrets. Those beliefs set us up for long-term, generational brokenness until we are able to finally identify them and find a place where we *can* talk, and trust, and feel.

For me, not acknowledging my feelings early in life and not being able to talk about the things that hurt me developed a pattern over time that would eventually cause me to crash and burn.

CHAPTER 2

Love and Loss

"Love does not begin and end the
way we seem to think it does.
Love is a battle, love is a war;
love is a growing up."
James A. Baldwin

R egardless of all we *don't* know during our growing up years, I am living proof that the choices we make from a faulty, unhealthy belief system can be redeemed. Good *can* come from them.

Marrying my husband, Jonas, is a decision I will never regret. He has been my rock and has modeled unconditional love in ways I never knew existed. But we had much to learn about having a healthy marriage when we first met as teenagers.

Jonas grew up in an Amish family from Lancaster County, but we never knew each other as children because his family was

Old Order Amish (as I mentioned previously, there was never any social interaction between Amish Mennonites and the Old Order Amish). My two sisters and I were friends with Jonas's brother, Sonny, who had left the Old Order Amish church when he was 16 and joined our Amish Mennonite Church. Sonny was a great name for him because he was funny, outgoing, and brought sunshine when he walked in a room. When Jonas turned 16, the time came for his father to give him his own carriage, which is the Amish custom. Getting his first carriage is a boy's rite of passage into adulthood. Jonas told his father he did not want a carriage. Instead, he wanted a car.

That decision, of course, marked his exit from the Amish lifestyle.

Jonas has fond memories of growing up Amish and recalls that there were many things he did not mind about his lifestyle as a kid. He didn't mind the plain clothes or living without electricity or phones. He just really loved cars. Jonas always puts it this way: "I didn't want a *horse*. I wanted *horsepower*."

Since his brother and sister both left the Old Order before him, it made it somewhat easier for Jonas to leave. Leaving—or being "English," as the Amish say—is never an easy step. Even though he and his brother were not shunned since they never officially joined the Old Order Church, it was still a difficult decision for them.

But if he hadn't left, we might never have had an opportunity to meet.

Shortly after leaving the Old Order, Jonas attended Sonny's birthday party, where my sisters and I met Jonas for the first time. He was quieter and more reserved than Sonny, but I remember thinking how handsome he was. (He still is.) My chance to get to know Jonas came during a game we often played called "Walk

A Mile." This was a safe, harmless way for girls and boys to meet one another. The boys and girls would pair up and "walk a mile" side by side until someone tapped them on the shoulder and asked to move up or back a place in line. At first, I was paired with Sonny. After we had walked and talked for a while, someone tapped me on the shoulder and asked me to move up two spaces. When I moved up, I found myself walking next to Jonas.

I still remember feeling giddy about walking next to him, but I tried not to make it too obvious. At first, I wasn't sure how to keep a conversation going with someone so quiet. I certainly didn't talk about emotions, but I could sure talk about plenty of other things and was considered quite the chatterbox. Yet, even I found myself struggling to keep the conversation flowing, although I enjoyed walking with him very much.

After getting acquainted during "Walk A Mile," Jonas invited me to attend a Happy Goodmans concert in Lancaster. I didn't tell him at the time, but another boy had already asked me to attend the same concert. I never wanted to break my word, so it would be a big deal for me to change my plans. But I couldn't bear to turn Jonas down. So, I gathered my courage, changed my plans, and chose Jonas. That was the beginning of our dating relationship.

During that time in our lives, my two sisters and I travelled from place to place singing almost every weekend. We were called The Triple Hearts Trio. Once we started dating, Jonas began making the drives with us and helped in any way he could whenever we sang together. We had been singing together since Fi, my youngest sister, was 11, I was 15, and our older sister, Becky, was 17 years old. It seemed as if we sang at every possible reunion, hospital, church, funeral, and wedding within driving distance of Lancaster County during those years. One of those years we counted no less than 28 weddings. Becky's boyfriend also came with us when we sang, and the five us ended up doing everything together. Much like our years growing up in busy Amish households, those hours together traveling, singing every Saturday night, Sunday morning, and often Sunday evenings, were constantly busy. And though we spent endless hours together, all of us were typically focused on *what* we were doing, rather than *how* we were doing. The busyness always kept conversation flowing, and Jonas's shyness became less of an obstacle for me as the uncomfortable silences started happening less often. Dating for two and a half years, Jonas and I had no idea we were about to face one of the most tragic crises of our life.

On a rare weekend off in August of 1967, several of us took a trip to the mountains. The weekend was filled with lots of laughter and joking around. Sonny and Jonas often played practical jokes on us when they were together, and that weekend was no exception. We didn't know those were the final hours of joy and laughter that we would experience with Sonny.

At the end of the weekend, Sonny left with his friend before the rest of us because they needed to be at work early Monday morning. Sonny and Jonas owned a body shop, and Jonas was planning to go back to work on Tuesday. But all of that changed when we received word in the wee hours of the morning that Sonny had been in an accident. He was on his motorcycle, about 500 yards from his shop, when a Mack truck loaded with stones hit him head-on.

Sonny was killed instantly.

The news fell on us like a bucket of ice water. Our drive home was spent in silence. Jonas and I sat in the back seat, and his sister and her boyfriend were taking turns driving. I could see Jonas crying off and on during the drive home, but there were no words to be said. Our hearts were broken, and Jonas was devastated.

Until that time, Sonny and Jonas had been inseparable. I'm sure Jonas wondered how he could ever function without his brother—and best friend—by his side. Sonny was always the life of the party. In the months that followed, his absence left a huge void in Jonas's life. And I wondered if he would ever be the same again.

Tragedy changes people. The honest truth is, his brother's death changed Jonas forever. His life has never been the same and Jonas still misses his brother fifty years later. Every once in a while, he wonders what life would be like if Sonny was still here. At the time of his death, Sonny's family grieved as the Amish always do. Hundreds of people from the community show up, grieve with the family, cook for the family, clean their house, and just sit with them. There are typically few words exchanged, but the experience of having a community surrounding you, grieving with you, is incredibly powerful in itself. Those despondent days are rich with reminders that you have a community that cares about you.

After those initial days, when everyone has gone home, the time comes to return to daily life. And in the midst of finding a new normal, the grief stays with you. The following Monday, Jonas was back at the shop, working all alone in silence. Grief was his constant companion. There were so many emotions that came with losing Sonny, but he simply did not have the words to express them.

Sonny's wife had lost her husband and two brothers within two and a half years. Jonas made it his mission to check in on her often and make sure she was okay. We often brought her with us when we sang on the weekends and spent a lot of time with her at home as well. Helping her seemed to give Jonas a sense of purpose that kept him from isolating himself during those difficult days. Jonas rarely spoke of his brother, yet the pain he was experiencing internally kept him closed off and quiet, even more so than before. I didn't know how to walk with him through this kind of pain. Neither of us had the ability to express our feelings in ways that could bring healing or closeness. We lived out the family rules, keeping a tight lid on those painful emotions, and silence during painful times would become a repeating theme in our life together.

The silence prevented the kind of connection I longed for with Jonas. I grieved for Sonny, but also for Jonas. Those feelings of loneliness brought up the feelings that I had experienced years earlier in the basement baking pies for the market, only much more intense. Other than the tears I shed in my family's basement kitchen, I hadn't cried for years until Sonny died. When the floodgates finally gave way, I cried for months—but only when I was alone. I prayed every day asking whether or not Jonas was really the man for me. I loved him, yet our relationship had become strained and uncomfortable because we could not talk about the grief or cry together. I knew his heart was broken and I wanted to fix it, but I knew this was something I could not fix. That reality was infinitely frustrating.

We had always been taught that when you face trouble, "Submit it to God and go on with your life." But that advice didn't comfort me this time. I felt as if part of Jonas was gone and lost forever. I was afraid he would never laugh again, that he would never be okay. I wondered every day if I should break up with him, but I could not bear the thought of ending the relationship, and just over a year after Sonny's accident, Jonas and I were married.

Looking back, I am overwhelmed with gratitude that we were able to stay together through those difficult circumstances. We had no idea how many more heartbreaks and deep waters there would be in the decades to come.

After Jonas and I were married, I began to attend a Bible study for women at the Mennonite Church. I felt more freedom there than I did at our Amish Mennonite church. The Amish and Amish Mennonite churches had strict rules about women's attire and did not permit women to cut their hair, but the Mennonite church was more lenient about our hair and clothing. Branching out from the Amish Mennonite church was the beginning of a slow transition for me from a life focused on rules and restrictions to an entirely different worship experience. While the differences were subtle, they were a refreshing, welcome change.

During the Bible studies and prayer times, I was not just learning information about God or hearing about the rules of the church and I began to experience a hunger for God I had never felt before. I learned about God's Spirit and how He helps us experience His love, guidance, and power. I started seeing evidence of Him all around me in ways I had never noticed before. I was driven to read the Bible and spend time in prayer. This new way of relating to God involved my emotions, which made me feel alive. I often came home and told Jonas about everything I was experiencing during the prayer times with these women. At first, he was worried about this new path I was on. The teaching was different from anything we had ever known, but he could see how this environment was helping me grow and, before long, he decided to attend a Bible study with me. The more involved we got, the more we looked forward to spending time with other believers and learning more about the Bible. My family was concerned about us and we began to feel some friction with them, yet

Jonas and I felt as if we were emerging together into a whole new way of life. For us, there was no going back.

Within a year, Fi, Becky, and Becky's husband, Aaron, had joined us. As a group, we became connected spiritually in a way none of us had ever experienced before. The religion we had experienced all our lives was replaced by a relationship with Christ. We grew up understanding religion as a set of rules, determined by man, that we had to live out perfectly. And if we didn't, there would be eternal consequences. There was no room for grace in religion.

So, when I began experiencing the teachings of Jesus with a new perspective, it changed my life. I was learning about love and grace. I was learning that faith isn't about a set of restrictions. I was learning about a God who loved and cherished me. It was personal. It was relational. It transformed me, and I became passionate about sharing this faith with others. The passion was infectious and, slowly, more family and friends began to attend with us.

My sisters and I sang together during these new and refreshing church gatherings. They started as a small group of 11 people, which quickly grew to 100, then continued growing. We knew we needed a building to accommodate the rapid growth. We had no money and knew nothing about starting a church, but by the early '70's, Victory Chapel was born, and we were meeting in a beautiful church that could seat more than 500 people. Word spread quickly about what was happening at Victory Chapel and we soon realized that we needed a pastor.

One weekend when my sisters and I were singing together in Texas, we met a vibrant pastor and were immediately drawn to him. Before long, he visited our church in Lancaster County, Pennsylvania, and was soon named the pastor at Victory Chapel. Everyone loved him, and the church seemed to be thriving under his leadership.

Our first daughter, LaWonna, was born during those years and Jonas and I were the happiest we had ever been. My sisters and I were singing together every week and the church was experiencing explosive growth. We were being led by this winsome pastor who had a gift for attracting more and more new members. Jonas and I became the youth pastors, and Becky's husband, Aaron, worked in the church office. Our family and friends' lives were intertwined. Words of affirmation and affection flowed freely between us. It was a totally new experience for us after spending years in an atmosphere where affection was never expressed outwardly. My sisters and I, who never remembered hearing the phrase "I love you" from our father, suddenly heard it constantly from our pastor and friends. Hugs were freely shared and the work of building this church together, week after week, was bonding for us. That sense of closeness and warmth filled a void inside me.

Before long, the church had grown to 1000 people. Our pastor eventually asked me and my sisters if we would consider singing exclusively at our church rather than traveling to other churches on the weekends. It was validating to hear that Pastor believed our role was so important to the weekly services that he wanted us there every week. We willingly agreed and no longer pursued other churches' invitations to sing.

One thing my family knew how to do well was work hard together, and for the first time our work was met with affirmation and appreciation. Our church became our whole life. Every single night for 13 weeks straight we attended revival. Now, I can see clearly how the isolated, pie-baking child inside me was so drawn to this environment. The hugs and words of gratitude I might have subconsciously longed to hear while working alone in that basement kitchen had become a part of my everyday landscape. Following our desire to build a church in the middle of Lancaster County had exceeded all of our expectations. We could never have imagined that we would build and then fill a church to overflowing on 10 acres of my dad's farm. It was beyond our wildest dreams. Having a role in building this church made my faith grow, and the excitement of it all made my emotions come alive.

Those good years were made even happier when I learned that I was going to have another baby. I gave birth to our second daughter, Angela, in 1974. For the next 19 months, life was exciting and happy. I was on a spiritual high and I couldn't get enough.

Sometimes I look back on those years building Victory Chapel as the happiest of my life. I believed that God was pleased with how my family and I were serving Him together and, in times like that, it can be so easy to start believing that if we are doing all the right things for Him, we will somehow get a special "pass" that exempts us from trouble or tragedy. The success of the church was bringing together people of all different backgrounds. There were so many members openly sharing their hard and troubled experiences with me and Jonas. We would listen and console to the best of our ability, but at that time in my life, I had no way of knowing how to relate to those who were struggling with shame, addiction, abuse, or depression.

I also had no way of knowing I was about to become one of them.

CHAPTER 3

The Story I Never Expected

*"There are wounds that never show
on the body that are deeper and more hurtful
than anything that bleeds."*
Laurell K. Hamilton

A ll I ever wanted—or expected—out of life was to have a happy family, and I was living that dream. Jonas and I were raising two delightful little girls and serving in our wonderful church together. We were surrounded by friends and family, our prayers were being answered, people were finding hope, and we were growing as people like never before.

September 8, 1975 started like any other day. The weather was beautiful and sunny. We had guests for breakfast that morning, and Jonas was planning to take them back to the church afterwards. As we were saying our goodbyes and they walked out the door, our daughter Angie slipped out as well. I was watching Jonas and our guests leave when I noticed that Angie was headed across the yard toward my parents' house. I thought about calling her back, but instead decided to call my mom and let her know Angie was on her way. I reached for the phone on our kitchen wall to let her know the girls were walking toward her house and that I would bring a change of clothes for Angie as soon as I got the kitchen cleaned up. I didn't even have the number dialed when I heard a scream from my father that I had never heard before, a scream of panic and terror. His screams were followed by a second wave of screaming. This time it was women's voices.

In that moment, I knew it was Angie.

Between mine and my parents' house was a barn where my dad made a type of house siding called permastone. My younger sister, Fi, was working for our father's masonry shop at the time and that morning she was mixing cement, which required the use of a Bobcat tractor. My brother and sister-in-law and their four children lived behind the shop, and Jonas and I lived in a double-wide trailer on the same property with our two girls. So Fi was always careful to watch for the kids whenever she was driving the tractor, especially when she was backing up. She looked back multiple times in each direction as she maneuvered the tractor that morning, just as she always did. But she knew something was terribly wrong when she caught a glimpse of our father waving both hands in the air, screaming, "Stop! Stop! Stop!"

Fi hit the brakes immediately, then looked down to see Angie's tiny body where the tractor wheels had just been.

She jumped off the tractor, so panicked that she forgot to put it into park and had to quickly jump back into the seat, so the tractor wouldn't continue rolling. Everyone who could hear the commotion rushed to see what was happening.

Everyone but me, that is.

When I heard the screams and commotion, I froze. I stood motionless in front of the phone with the receiver dangling from the wall. I couldn't move or breathe. I began walking in circles in my kitchen, pulling my hair, saying, "No, God. No, God. Not Angie!"

When I finally summoned the strength to go to the door and look out, my father was running toward me carrying Angie's tiny, motionless body in his arms. He kept repeating, "I think she's dead! I think she's dead!"

I couldn't speak. I couldn't even reach for her. So, he laid her in the grass on the front lawn. I stared with disbelief at her seemingly perfect little frame, not even bleeding anywhere. I just couldn't take it in. Suddenly, all I wanted to do was run. I ran back and forth through the yard pulling my hair. I didn't want to leave her, or I would have run for miles and miles, as far away as I could get. Instead, I picked her up and ran and was overwhelmed by the need to rush her to the clinic. Surely, they could do something for her! I ran with her in my arms to my dad's car and my dad followed. On the three-minute ride to the clinic, I was holding her. I wanted to look at her but kept having to look away. It was all too much.

I walked into the clinic with Angie, laid her up on the counter and told the receptionist, "I think she's dead."

We were quickly rushed into a treatment room, where I waited alone with Angie. Her body looked so small lying on the examination table. A doctor and nurse came in to look at her ... but there wasn't anything to be done. The doctor pulled a white sheet over Angie and left the room. The nurse stayed for a brief time, and then I was left alone in the room, waiting for Jonas to arrive. I was still in my bathrobe when Jonas got there. When he saw the look on my face, he knew. He held me, and we sobbed together. Then I asked him if he would pray that Jesus would bring her back to life. Jonas asked, "… do we really want to bring Angie back to pain and suffering?"

———————

I learned later that when everyone else rushed to Angie's aid, Fi's reaction to the trauma was to climb off the tractor in a panicky daze and hide. She watched us drive off toward the clinic with Angie but stayed hidden in the tall grass beside our parents' barn all alone, weeping.

In moments like that, the brain doesn't keep track of time. Its sole purpose is simply helping us survive. Fi doesn't know how long she sat there before our sister Becky and our pastor's wife found her and walked her to the house, whether it was minutes or hours later. The shock, the overwhelming sense of pain, guilt, and sadness, the questions and horror of it all hit the whole family like a tidal wave. Fi was curled up on the couch rocking back and forth with a pillow over her head when we got back from the clinic. She was afraid to show her face because she was sure Jonas and I hated her for what happened, although we assured her over and over that we didn't hate her or even blame her. We knew how much she loved Angie. Fi's wedding was two months away at the time of the accident, and Angie was supposed to be her flower girl. Her memory of Angie's accident is heartbreaking as she recalls what happened inside her.

The day Angie was killed was the day I said, 'I am
not going to let myself feel anything anymore.' It's
like I put all my feelings into a two-quart jar, put

the lid on, and put it away. I didn't cry for years after that. Looking back, I would do things differently with the wedding coming so soon after the accident. I would have stopped the train and gotten off. I would have gotten help and gone to counseling. In that culture, we didn't stop or get help. So, we went through with the wedding. I was such an unhappy bride.

No medicine or doctor could fix our shattered hearts. Our family had no language for processing this kind of pain, no way to say out loud the things we were feeling, and no idea how this loss would shape us for the rest of our lives. Those unspoken rules kicked in at a whole new level: *don't talk, don't trust, don't feel.* We had become experienced at ignoring bad feelings, and that's all we knew to do. We prayed for peace and tried to move forward.

Angela's funeral was on a Thursday. The next Sunday, Fi, Becky, and I were back to singing in front of our church. Fi went on with her wedding two months later, even though she was devastated. We all struggled to just carry on with life. I thought God would be honored if I could show my church community how strong I was by going on with life as usual. That may sound crazy, but I thought that was my only option if I claimed to be someone who put her faith in God. I knew how to busy myself and push aside my feelings. After all, I had been doing that my whole life. So, I went through the motions of my daily life, while trying to hold back waves of grief the size of Niagara Falls.

Lurking in the back of my mind was an unfamiliar feeling that I kept trying to push down. I had never before understood how a person could be angry with God, yet I suddenly couldn't comprehend why He would take Angie from us. Jonas and I were serving him. My heart was to please Him.

How could He let this happen?

I wondered how He could let this happen to Fi, who loved Angie so much. How would she ever make it through this? How would any of us survive?

No amount of work ethic, or faith, or self-discipline could console me. And then guilt would crop up for questioning God like that. I was taught to never question authority, especially the Ultimate Authority. I still had so much to learn about His grace and how He can meet us in our pain rather than judging us for it.

As a result of our pain, a deafening silence fell between me and Jonas. I didn't want to burden him with my pain. He, too, lost a daughter. And only a few years earlier, he lost the brother he loved so much. The last thing I wanted to do was off-load my heartache onto his already heavy heart. So, our collective, unspoken sorrow built up between us, forming a wall that neither of us knew how to change.

As days turned to weeks and months after Angie's accident, I had no relief from the grief and I was surprised. I had no idea that trauma and grief cannot be prayed away and felt more isolated every day. Trying to stay busy with church suddenly had no meaning for me. The high, the excitement, the lives being changed … none of that mattered to me. I was confused by everything I was feeling and constantly asked God one question over and over: "Why?"

There was nothing that could fill the void of our busy nineteen-month-old, my child who suddenly didn't need me anymore. I felt as if the curtains of my soul were drawn forever. There was no way I could go back to the life I knew before, and I didn't know how to move forward. Until then, I believed that when problems came along, I could simply surrender them to God and He would take the pain away. I didn't understand that grief is a long process that doesn't end with a funeral. I cried in secret and continued surrendering my pain to God through sobs and anguish. When it was time to make dinner, I would dry my tears and make dinner. When it was time to go to church, I would dry my tears and go to church. When it was time to go to bed at night, I would sleep on the couch so that Jonas wouldn't see me crying. I kept thinking if I could just say the right prayer, relief would come.

Five months later, I still didn't understand why I didn't feel any better than the day she died. I was embarrassed to tell anyone that my grief was not getting any better, so whenever I went out, I pushed it down. The energy it took to keep pushing the pain down kept me feeling constantly defeated. My soul was crushed. At that time, I believed that all these ongoing painful emotions meant that I was spiritually flawed. I didn't have per-mission, as far back as I can remember, to verbalize or show any kind of pain or sadness. That belief ran deep and added a layer of shame to my pain. Pretending that I wasn't grieving or that I didn't need to grieve only added to the pain. Rather than healing from the grief, I felt as if I was dying.

Today, I understand that grieving is a process God has created to help us heal from a terrible loss or trauma. Every emotion that I was trying to reign back was one He gave me to help process the pain. He gives us emotions as a healthy release for pain that our bodies aren't meant to continue to carry. The grieving process is healthy, even when it is hard. And grieving together, as a couple, is possible. Jonas and I just didn't know how at the time.

I recently learned of a young couple, Michael and Maggie, who lost their baby girl. Her name was Willow, and she died very suddenly the same day she was born. She seemed perfectly healthy at birth, then simply stopped breathing four hours later. The trauma of losing her so unexpectedly was devastating and they asked all the same questions others who lose children always ask themselves, myself included.

Was this my fault?
Could I have done something to prevent this?
Why would God allow this to happen
to an innocent child?
Did I do something to deserve this?

They received wise counsel that I wish Jonas and I had received when Angie passed. Michael and Maggie were advised to talk openly and frequently with each other about how they were doing. They initially felt the same fear I had about sharing my pain with Jonas. They didn't want to bring each other down even more by sharing their sorrow. Yet they followed that wise counsel and allowed each other a safe space where they could process their feelings about missing their sweet daughter. And rather than multiplying the grief, sharing it gave them each great comfort. Talking about Willow and keeping her memory alive in their daily life played an essential role in their ability to find joy again. Today, their marriage is stronger than it was before Willow's birth.

Today, Jonas and I are finally able to speak freely about our little girl. And just as Michael and Maggie will never stop missing Willow, Jonas and I will never stop missing our Angie. We wonder what she would be like now and share a strange mix of feelings when we consider how tragic it was to lose her, and yet, how much we have grown and changed as a result of that once-inconsolable pain. Our children can teach us so much, even when they're no longer with us.

CHAPTER 4

A Trauma Worse Than Death

"Death is not the worst that can happen …"
Plato

My life, as I knew it, was over. I wanted more than anything to rewind time, back to the days before Angie died. Knowing I could never do that left me feeling out of control. There was often a restlessness inside me, a fear that something else terrible could happen at any moment. All the excitement, answered prayers, and growth Jonas and I experienced in the years prior to Angie's accident felt like a distant memory as I trudged through the weeks and months that followed. I did my best to move forward, without seeking guidance from anyone to help me work through the grief. The grief came in waves and, every now and then, a wave would knock me down.

So, I did what I always did. I prayed, hoping and believing God would hear me and answer my prayers. I was convinced that God answered prayers. I had seen Him do that so many times. I kept waiting for Him to relieve me from my emotional distress, my confusion and sadness. I didn't understand that when we experience trauma, our minds and emotions are ignited and that everything I was feeling was completely normal. In my mind, I only understood God wasn't answering my prayer.

I was angry, hopeless, and doubtful of everything I'd ever believed. I still believed God was with me, but I couldn't understand how He fit into my pain and suffering. I started questioning His role in all the suffering in the world—thoughts I'd never struggled with before.

I was deep in a world that, even to this day, I find hard to describe. I'd never before understood why anyone would question God. I believed He was sovereign and that whatever happened was His will, so I didn't know why I should bother asking, "Why, God?" Yet I found myself living with that question twenty-four hours, seven days a week. Not only did I *understand* why those questions plagued people who live with pain and suffering, but I was one of them. In my despair, I cried out to God, begging Him to send me someone, anyone I could talk to. Although I felt weak even praying for help, I longed to talk to someone who understood, perhaps another woman who had been through the loss of a child and could help me process my overwhelming waves of grief.

One weekend, I went to the altar to pour out my heart to God, the only public place where I would let myself cry. I felt safe there and I prayed for peace. I asked God to help me through all my confusion.

As I prayed that Sunday, our Pastor came up and prayed for me. I was desperate for consolation and appreciated his reassuring words. After his prayer over me, he said, "You know I love you, Anne."

Growing up, the words, "I love you," were saved only for God. They were sacred. But in this new church setting, words of love and affirmation flowed freely. I was growing more comfortable with hearing and saying those words, but then Pastor said something I didn't quite understand.

He said, "Anne, I love you in a special way."

And then he invited me to come to his office the next week, so we could talk further. Pastor's leadership was resulting in dynamic growth in our church. He was a powerful speaker and people responded by the hundreds to his messages. Entire families were experiencing life change together under his influence. So, it was a gift for me to be invited to learn from him at a time when I was so desperate for perspective and guidance. I was grateful that my prayer for someone to talk to had been answered so quickly. In the back of my mind, there was a small question mark as I wondered what "a special way" meant, but I dismissed my apprehension because I knew I needed help. I couldn't go on without talking to someone about the sadness that was threatening to swallow me up.

When I told Jonas that I was going to talk with our pastor that week, he was glad I was seeking help from someone we trusted. Two days later, I met Pastor in his office and, for the first time since Angie's death, I felt complete freedom to say whatever I needed to say. I spoke openly about the pain I had bottled up for so long and about how difficult it was for me and Jonas to process our grief together. Pastor consoled me and listened patiently, without judgment. I was overwhelmed by his warmth and acceptance. What a relief it was to hear that he believed in me and was committed to helping me through this crisis.

And then he said something that felt strange, like a dagger in my heart. He told me that Jonas would never be able to understand my pain or meet my needs and that seemed to answer a question I had secretly struggled with as I wondered if Jonas and I would ever be able to have the relationship we once had. Pastor's words felt true and he assured me that he could help me get through this. At the end of that first meeting, he prayed over me.

Then he preyed on me.

As I got up to leave, he stood up from behind his desk and walked around to where I was standing. He gave me a big hug, which was not unusual. Hugs were freely exchanged at our church. But then he kissed me, and I was shocked and repulsed. I didn't know what to do. I'm sure I did not respond in the way he was hoping for. I was already grieving the death of my 19-month-old daughter, but I felt a different kind of pain in that moment. I felt dirty. I left his office quietly, totally bewildered, and promised myself I would never tell anyone what happened. I was sure nobody would believe me even if I did say something. I don't have many memories of the days and weeks that followed other than that I told no one. Everyone loved him and thought he was a good man and I didn't want to further isolate myself. I was too fragile to take that risk.

Pastor and I continued to meet, just to talk, and his words haunted me. What did he mean when he said that he could meet my needs? What I needed was a respite from the isolation and confusion, so believing he understood brought me great comfort and freed me to talk openly about the deeply painful feelings I didn't think I could entrust to anyone else. The relief that came from sharing my grief openly with Pastor was something I didn't think I could survive without.

Once again, I didn't grasp that the overwhelming sadness, anger, disbelief, questions, depression, and guilt were normal emotions for anyone experiencing grief. The traumatic way in which Angie died created extra layers of emotional pain for me, as well as physical symptoms that are now widely known as Post Traumatic Stress Disorder (PTSD). I couldn't accurately express what I was feeling since I didn't even know if I should have those feelings in the first place.

A therapist told me many years later:

"Alone, we die. Connected, we live."

And that is so very true. I felt as if I would die without the comfort I received from Pastor during our conversations. After months of receiving his support and counsel, I was grateful. But as my dark cloud of grief slowly began to lift, I felt a different kind of darkness settling in. I felt guilty about how dependent I had become on the pastor for emotional support. That connection had become my lifeline.

When Jonas and I learned that we were expecting our third daughter, LaVale, I was thrilled about having another baby to hold. However, Pastor's response to the news bewildered me. He was angry when he learned that I was expecting. He said he didn't think I was ready for another child.

Those words were so painful to hear when I thought he would be happy for us. I thought he cared about me and Jonas. In my naivety, I never guessed that he might have motives other than to be supportive.

After months of having coffee and talking frequently, my emotional connection to Pastor grew stronger and stronger. I tried to be clear that I was not interested in a physical or romantic relationship, in spite of the strong emotional bond I felt. But I couldn't have possibly predicted how much control he would try to gain over my life, or that the real reason he was upset with my pregnancy was sinister.

One morning, Pastor and I met at a restaurant to talk, as we often did. Before we left, he told me he wanted to take me somewhere. I got in his car, wondering what this was all about.

He drove me to a hotel in another town.

I was beyond confused. I was a wife and mother, and I was four months pregnant. I still remember walking into the hotel wearing dark green maternity pants with a light green top, feeling the weight of my growing tummy, and wondering why I was there, still not getting it.

It was there, after months of giving me the connection *I* needed, that Pastor demanded I give him what *he* wanted. He raped me for the first time that day. We spent just enough time in that room for a cold, transactional act that left me feeling terrified, lost, and utterly trapped. He had crossed a line that left me feeling like there was no way out. Everything changed.

During the quiet drive back to the restaurant, where my car was still parked, he assured me that if I told anyone, they would never believe me.

A few months later, I had the joy of holding our third baby girl, Joy LaVale. And as I look back, I am grateful that even a calculating predator could not rob me and Jonas of our beautiful daughter. She was such a gift to me during those dark days.

Her birth gave me another reason to hold our family together, although I struggled to do that well. The turmoil inside of me only heightened as Pastor's abuse consumed more and more of my time and energy.

For the next six years, I remained trapped in this abusive relationship with a sexual predator. I spent every day looking for a way out. I slowly came to realize that his offering to counsel me through my grief was never really about understanding me or helping me overcome the grief. It was all part of his plan to ensnare me. He knew exactly what he was doing, and he knew how to twist the truth and confuse me with guilt, fear, shame, and lies until I was too lost in the darkness to find my way out. This pastor, seemingly devoted to speaking truth from the platform on Sundays, effectively convinced me not to tell anyone what he was doing, not to trust anyone but him, and not to listen to the warnings I felt in my gut.

Those toxic rules were at play again:
don't talk, don't trust, don't feel.

Pastor convinced me that I was fully responsible for his actions. I had no frame of reference for this strange relationship. At that time, I imagined that sexual abuse would be easy to identify, probably involving a sudden, violent attack from a stranger. I would have fought with every ounce of my strength if the abuse had been that obvious, but it was disorienting to be coerced into a sexual relationship I didn't want by someone I trusted and admired, using my own grief as bait. I thought nothing could hurt more than Angie's death. But the pain of this relationship—which I had mistaken for an answer to my prayers—led me further down a path of confusion and shame that drove me deeper than ever into despair. There was no one I felt safe to tell.

As time went on, I expended endless efforts covering up and protecting a relationship I hated. I hid behind the activities of daily life, hoping no one could see how deeply depressed and detached I had become. I cannot count the times I became convinced I could not survive another day. I honestly believed dying was the only way I could escape the pain. Yet, I was also convinced that taking my own life would prevent me from spending eternity with Angie.

According to decades of studies, abuse and suicidal tendencies often go hand-in-hand. Addiction is also closely linked to abuse because victims long for relief and, if they cannot find a healthy outlet, turn to self-medication. To be abused and trapped in secrecy is a kind of suffering we are simply not meant to endure. Suicide and addiction seem to offer the one thing we most want: an escape. More than anything in the world, I wanted a way out—no matter how that escape came.

Looking back, I am relieved I did not follow through with those thoughts of ending my life. Escaping this world would have robbed me of the healing process and would have left my girls without a mother. I would never have had the chance to mend my relationship with Jonas, to watch my girls grow into strong women, or to find any semblance of peace. I would have missed the chance to share my story with other women so they, too, might find a way to rewrite their endings. I would have missed out on an incredible future and success I couldn't possibly have predicted.

Before I knew any measure of hope or happiness was possible for me, I was convinced that I was unforgivable, unchangeable, and unlovable. That wasn't true, of course. But it *felt* true.

It is impossible to adequately paint a picture of how twisted and strange those years became. The control Pastor had over me, the lies, confusion, and jealousy, the perversion and constant manipulation all made my world seem very small. Pastor seemed to always know where I was, and everywhere I went, he was there.

Somehow, I knew that I had no control over Angie's death. Although I would never stop missing her or grieving, I could eventually accept that it was an accident and she was no longer experiencing the pain of this world. This unexpected and confusing relationship with my pastor, on the other hand, who was a well-respected man from all appearances, was a trauma worse than death.

CHAPTER 5

Identifying Trauma

God has mercifully ordered that the
human brain works slowly;
first the blow, hours afterwards the bruise.
Walter de la Mare, *The Return*

The brain sends warning signals when a threat is present. I didn't realize how the trauma of Angie's death had altered my brain on a cellular level. That's what trauma does to everyone's brain who experiences it, but I didn't know anything about trauma back then. Like an internal Homeland Security Department, the brain knows when a threat is present and remembers it for the rest of our lives. When the brain sends its warning signals, one of three responses is triggered: fight, flight, or freeze—reactions as automatic as blinking.

LaWonna vividly remembers a day when, out of nowhere, her brain remembered the trauma of Angie's accident.

One beautiful sunny day, I was walking out of the house, saying goodbye to the kids, heading to work. At that time, there was major construction going on near our home. As I was waving goodbye to the kids, out of the corner of my eye, I saw Mia, who was almost two years old, playing on the swings ... and about 50 feet behind her I saw a Bobcat tractor, one that looked just like the one that killed my sister.

In reality, Mia was in no danger at all. But what I saw in my head was this Bobcat coming right at her and I literally fell to the ground and completely lost it. I seriously lost it!

Feelings and memories flooded in, including many of the missing pieces I thought were gone forever from my memory. I was completely paralyzed both physically and emotionally. This storm had been quietly brewing for most of my life, and finally let loose.

I became irate—seriously pissed. All the years I spent pretending everything was fine instantly transformed into rage. For the first time in my life, I couldn't flip the switch back to calm.

Until that day, I didn't know exactly what LaWonna witnessed the day of Angie's accident. She never talked about it. But her mind and body carried that memory inside her for 30 years until the sight of Mia in front of the Bobcat brought it to the surface.

———————◆———————

Abuse adds another layer to trauma, and it is far more common than I ever knew. One of every three females experiences sexual trauma, as does one of every six males.[1] Even those staggering statistics are probably low since abuse frequently goes unreported. Those numbers include religious and church settings. Even within Amish communities, where the goal is to create a protected culture of simple living, untouched by a corrupt world, sex abuse still happens. It is important for both men and women to understand what to look for and what to do if they find themselves caught in a relationship that is not safe.

I want others to have the information I lacked.

There are people who don't believe a woman can be unaware that she is being abused. I can tell you, without hesitation, that I was trapped in a toxic, sexually abusive relationship for six years without having any idea what to call it. I know now what I experienced is called clergy sexual abuse.

Let me also say that not being able to identify the abuse at the time it was happening in no way protected me from the damage it caused. Not knowing actually heightened my pain because I believed I was responsible for the way the relationship went. One moment, I would feel threatened by the relationship, and the next I'd argue with myself, "But he is my pastor, he is helping me through my grief ..."

Abuse takes many forms. We often think of physical abuse, which is the easiest to identify. But more subtle forms of abuse, like verbal and psychological abuse, inflict fear, doubt, and mental anguish from threats, including:

- ✦ **Clergy abuse**: the misuse of power and trust that comes with being a spiritual leader and may or may not include sexual or physical abuse.
- ✦ **Spiritual abuse**: involves using Biblical phrases, spiritual language, false guilt or fear

of hell to manipulate, intimidate, and control others' behaviors

✦ **Abuse of power**: the use of someone's authority (spiritual or otherwise) to inflict pain or personal agendas at another person's cost.

Often these forms of abuse overlap, isolating their victims. All abuse involves an imbalance of power. Abusers and predators invariably establish a high level of control, often gradually, over time. When qualities admired early in a relationship—like attentiveness, generosity, and protectiveness—turn into controlling and frightening behaviors, that's a symptom indicating that an abusive pattern is developing. That pattern might present itself in a few isolated incidents at first, which the abuser apologizes for and promises never to do again. But the pattern will always reappear and become increasingly more frequent and more severe, just like my relationship with Pastor progressed.

I wish I had known the signs of abuse at the time.

The Mayo Clinic*[2] provides a list of warning signs to watch for in any kind of relationship, which is provided below. Both men and women can suffer from abuse, so regardless of gender, you might be experiencing domestic abuse if your partner has demonstrated any of the following behaviors:

✦ Calls you names, insults you or puts you down

✦ Prevents you from going to work or school

✦ Stops you from seeing family members or friends

✦ Tries to control how you spend money, where you go, or what you wear

✦ Acts jealous or possessive or constantly accuses you of being unfaithful

+ Gets angry when drinking alcohol or using drugs
+ Threatens you with violence or a weapon
+ Hits, kicks, shoves, slaps, chokes or otherwise
  hurts you, your children, or your pets
+ Forces you to have sex or engage in sexual acts
  against your will
+ Blames you for his or her violent behavior or
  tells you that you deserve it

It also important to keep in mind that *coercion* is not the same as *consent*. Guilt trips or repeated advances after you say "no" are red flags and trauma begins the minute you can't say "no." Someone who cannot accept that answer cannot be trusted as a safe partner who loves and respects you.

I remember feeling stupid for trusting someone who was ultimately hurtful. I believed it was my fault. Abusers invariably try to place responsibility on the other person and as a result of Pastor's manipulation, I developed unhealthy patterns that kept me bound to him. While my conscious thoughts did not have a category for what was happening, my brain knew I was not safe and was trying to send warning signals. I had no room in my brain for thoughts about how I could live out my hopes and dreams, have a great family, or nurture my marriage to the man of my dreams. The toxic relationship was running my life and keeping me constantly preoccupied. I now identify that as "survival mode." All I could hope for was to keep from falling apart on any given day.

A relationship with an abuser will never change for the better. Abusers cannot stop hurting people on their own. So many people hope things will get better if they are patient, but the pattern of an abuser is always a dead end. Predators are particularly dangerous because they use non-consensual and even illegal means of satisfying their compulsions. Their behaviors are never limited to one person and escalate over time. Not every abuser is a predator, but every sexual predator is an abuser. Examples of predatory behavior include the use of power or a professional status to obtain sex, confinement, pursuing sexual relationships with minors or mentally disabled adults, child pornography, rape, and other non-consensual acts. Predators typically have sexual addictions, although not every sex addict is a predator. Both engage in compulsive sexual behavior, but non-predatory sex addicts are only willing to engage in legal, consensual sex. Predators, however, stop at nothing.

My pastor's use of his professional role to coerce victims into non-consensual sex clearly marked him as a predator. He demonstrated many other signs as the relationship progressed but let me be clear that his unwillingness to take "no" for an answer was the most glaring warning sign that he was a predator.

That remains the *only* sign anyone ever needs to call abuse by its proper name.

In a reciprocal, healthy relationship, sex is never forced or demanded. But a predator will never stop demanding until he gets his way, using intimidation, guilt, or threats to make his prey feel afraid to say "no." Even if he initially uses tenderness and says all the things his victim wants to hear, manipulation into an unwanted sexual relationship is *not* the same as consent. It is essential to recognize why your brain is sending danger signals and identify abuse in order to find your way to safety and healing.

Diane R. Garland was one of the first people I learned about who studied and wrote specifically about clergy sexual abuse. Her work has been so important to me as I continue coming to terms with this phenomenon. Clergy abuse has been happening for centuries yet, for obvious reasons, has rarely been discussed. Garland's article, "When Wolves Wear Shepherds' Clothing…" details exactly what clergy abuse is and why it is so difficult to identify. She sheds light on why this kind of abuse can be so confusing.

> *The reality of clergy sexual abuse of adults…is a more difficult issue to understand… There is the assumption that if both are adults and there is no physical coercion, then the relationship is consensual. In fact, however, when persons with power— social workers, counselors, pastors, seminary professors and administrators, pastoral and clinical supervisors, and religious employers—attempt to seduce into sexual relationships those over whom they have power, the relationship is not consensual. More than other professional roles, the ministry is liable to the blurring of roles because friendships do develop in a faith community, and the boundaries between professional and social time are often unclear.* [*3]

I was not a seductress looking for an affair when I went to Pastor for help. I was a grieving woman looking for a safe place to find wholeness. Never, in a million years, would I have walked into my pastor's office wanting or expecting that hour to end as it did. And I certainly couldn't have imagined that it would lead to being raped and trapped in the nightmare which, even still today, causes painful repercussions in my life.

Like blood in water, wounded people trigger the internal radar of a predator. The pattern of behavior when a predator finds a potential victim is chillingly predictable and deceptive. I can look back now and recognize red flags I didn't see then, such as the pastor turning me against my husband to increase his influence over me. He constantly tried to deepen my dependence on him for emotional support for leverage. Pastor called our relationship an affair so, because I trusted him, I believed it was an affair. I lived with constant shame and self-loathing for allowing it to happen, thinking that I just wasn't strong enough to break free, which is exactly what he wanted me to believe.

When I think about it, I'm not sure my abuser even understood that he was a predator. He might have been shocked and offended by such a label. However, it is important to understand that even if a predator does not know what to call his or her damaging behavior, the truth comes out through their actions, patterns, and the pain they cause. Regardless of his awareness of his motives, his predatory instincts were finely tuned and brought indescribable pain.

The grooming process is one tactic that predators use to carefully build trust and increase their victims' dependence on them. Eventually, I could see how he had begun grooming me years earlier. Long before he actually forced me, he patiently used each encounter we had to strengthen my loyalty to him, telling me things I was desperate to hear and creating a bond I wouldn't be strong enough to break. He would make sure he got what he wanted. His gradual approach, blurring the lines between pastor and congregant little by little, was deceptive and intentional. I later also learned about trauma bonding, which explains my confusing dependence on him. Abusers intend to make sure victims are constantly reminded how much they need him or her, so the victim is convinced that survival would not be bearable without the abuser. The power an abuser gets from this dependence further fuels their insatiable desire for more and that bond keeps both the victim and abuser dependent on one another, in spite of the pain inflicted on the victim.

Without healing, trauma bonds can keep a victim trapped indefinitely and even make him or her feel the weight of responsibility for the problematic relationship. Trauma bonding is not something we do on purpose. The bonds formed between victims and abusers are powerful, even when victims know deep inside that the relationship is not healthy. If a victim does find a way to safety, those bonds may still cause a similar kind of relationship in the future time and time again. That's one of many reasons why leaving an abusive relationship must be followed by an intentional path toward healing and wholeness.

No one can navigate that path alone.

Predators do not come into our lives with warning labels. Protecting ourselves and our families means knowing what to watch for and refusing to accept abuse in any form. Protecting ourselves and others against abuse also means understanding that abuse is a crime.

YES—abuse is a crime.

Beware of anyone who undermines your trust in the people who love you. Watch for signs that someone is trying to control you or is creating an environment of dependence on himself or herself. If you are not safe, your brain will try to warn you. Learn to recognize and pay attention to those warnings. Healthy relationships never use control or manipulation. A safe person allows you the freedom to speak truthfully, express your emotions without fear, and enjoy reciprocal trust. If you suspect that you are being drawn into a potentially harmful relationship, even if it is meeting a need, believe me when I say the longer you wait to leave, the more damage will be done to you and to everyone you care about.

I recently read the following passage and realized it describes predators in accurate detail. It reminded me that predators and abusers have been making their mark for centuries.

> *Their mouths are full of cursing, lies, and threats.*
> *Trouble and evil are on the tips of their tongues.*
>> *They lurk in ambush in the villages,*
>> *waiting to murder innocent people.*
>> *They are always searching for helpless victims.*
>> *Like lions crouched in hiding,*
>> *they wait to pounce on the helpless.*
>> *Like hunters they capture the helpless*
>> *and drag them away in nets.*
> *Their helpless victims are crushed;*
>> *they fall beneath the strength of the wicked.*
>> *The wicked think, "God isn't watching us!*
>> *He has closed his eyes and won't even see what*
>> *we do!"*
> *Arise, O Lord!*
>> *Punish the wicked, O God!*
>> *Do not ignore the helpless!*
> *Why do the wicked get away with despising God?*
>> *They think, "God will never call us to account."*
> *But you see the trouble and grief they cause.*
>> *You take note of it and punish them.*
>> *The helpless put their trust in you.*

> *You defend the orphans.*
> *Break the arms of these wicked, evil people!*
> *Psalm 10:7-15 (NLT)*

We must be aware.

CHAPTER 6

Lies That Keep Us Stuck

"What kills a soul? Exhaustion, secret keeping,
image management.
And what brings a soul back from the dead?
Honesty, connection, grace."
Shauna Niequist, *Present Over Perfect*

Since predators rarely abuse just one person, you might have guessed by now that I was not the only woman who was coerced into a relationship with Pastor. I'm not sure exactly how or when I came to the realization that he was seeing both of my sisters at the same time he was seeing me, but, somehow, I knew.

Of course, we never talked about it. I see how we must have been ideal targets—naïve women who didn't want any trouble, broken women who had experienced a tragedy that weakened our resolve, women longing for connection, women who had been well-trained to never *talk*, never *feel*, and never *trust*.

At first, he gave the impression I could talk openly to him, express my feelings, and trust him completely. Eventually something clicked, and I realized I could not trust him at all. But by then I was so ensnared that leaving seemed an impossible feat.

Over time, his behaviors escalated. When he began trying to bring multiple women together at once, there was no doubt that he was seeing numerous women simultaneously. I'm not sure we will ever know how many other women were caught in his toxic addiction. I somehow escaped those orgies, but not because he didn't repeatedly try to involve me.

Earlier, when he convinced my sisters and I not to sing at other churches, he was starting to control where we went and what we did. His attempts to keep us close, compliant, and under his control were early warnings that we didn't know to watch for. There were very specific lies that kept my sisters and I imprisoned in that relationship, to the detriment of every other relationship in our lives, such as:

+ I cannot tell anyone.
+ It is all my fault.
+ No one will understand.
+ If I tell, I will lose everything.
+ There is no way out.
+ God is displeased with me.

I was completely paralyzed by those lies, which Pastor constantly reinforced. When I decided I would tell no one about the relationship, I thought it was for my own safety and protection. But in reality, those lies only served to protect him and destroy me. The very lies that shielded him from consequences were eating away at my marriage. He was a master in the art of manipulation and made sure I felt too ashamed to blow his cover.

One by one, as each of us became trapped in his web, we started spending less time with each other. My sisters and I agree that he was intent on tearing us apart. He was constantly trying to shift our loyalty, hoarding it for himself, until we were emotionally isolated from each other and our spouses. As long as we believed the lies Pastor perpetuated, we suffered in silence. Yet we lived in close proximity to one another, going to the same church, singing together every Sunday. We were inseparable our whole lives until these chasms grew between us. That's what keeping secrets does; it cuts off the sense of connection we most need.

My older sister, Becky, suffered the longest. She spent 10 years under the influence of Pastor's abuse and recalls how relentlessly he tried to draw her into a sexual relationship. Over and over again she refused his advances. Twice she even brought her Bible to him and pointed to scripture that specifically addressed the immorality he was suggesting and each time he "interpreted" the verses for her, twisting their meaning and confusing her. He used his status as a pastor to convince her that she needed his "wisdom." That kind of spiritual abuse is dangerous and cunning, and he did not quit until he had brainwashed her into believing that he cared for her and she could not survive without him. Their relationship caused her an overwhelming sense of guilt because she *knew* right from wrong and *still* could not escape his trap. He even made her believe she was equally responsible for what was happening.

Fi was next. He pressured her for a long time, beginning six months before she was married. She remembers his verbal abuse long before any sexual abuse. She kept his advances at bay for at least a year, but he was relentless.

A few months into her marriage, the dark cloud of guilt and pain surrounding Angie's death overshadowed everything. Her new marriage was suffering almost as much as her own soul. That is when Pastor swept in and made his move. He was well practiced with appealing to women in vulnerable times when they were least prepared to continue saying "no" to his relentless advances.

My sisters and I all experienced various forms of abuse from him at one time or another—verbal, spiritual, sexual, and emotional—but especially damaging to Fi was the psychological abuse. She was tortured by his lies that caused her overwhelming fear and anguish. Pastor was cunning. He knew exactly how to get to us and used that knowledge mercilessly, which is exactly how he trapped me. Like a hawk hunting for his next meal, watching the ground for injured prey, he swept in when I didn't have any fight left and knew exactly how to keep me from slipping out of his controlling grasp.

Knowing our abuser was married with children, discovering that he was involved in simultaneous sexual relationships (with women who were also married with children), you might think we would have run to the authorities and had him removed from the church immediately.

**But the secrecy was far too blinding …
the lies too convincing.**

Those lies were based in zero truth, yet we believed them fully. Life with a predator is confusing. You hate him, but also feel connected to him. You believe him, but can't fully trust him. You stay when you don't want to stay.

None of us understood the trauma we were experiencing or the full extent of the damage it was doing until much later. The path of least resistance, for the sake of survival, was to stay quiet. We were bound to our perpetrator as long as we believed his lies.

———————

Six years of secrecy piled on top of the devastating loss of my daughter took a terrible toll on me both physically and emotionally. My marriage was struggling more than ever. I had two young daughters to care for, yet I could barely function. I was navigating life in a fog of depression with no guidance, no one I could trust, and constant lies to keep the horrible truth from further unraveling my life. Leaving my abuser was something I wanted and needed to do. But I kept believing the lies. There may be a different list of lies that keeps others stuck in their pain, but everyone caught in the mire of secrecy will remain there as long as they continue to believe things that aren't true.

When lies trigger our deepest fears and insecurities, they seem bigger than they really are. Those of us who hear those lies in a church setting are also forced to reconcile them with our understanding of God. Anyone claiming to represent God is accountable to Him for the words they say and the lies they tell—people we are supposed to be able to trust.

I have a good friend, Sue, who believed she could never leave her abuser because she thought she was happily married to him. The abuse started happening ever so slowly, much like the proverbial frog in the pot of boiling water, and it coincided with her husband's spiral into prescription drug abuse and pornography. His manipulation of Scripture placed the blame on her and the shame she felt was unbearable. In addition, she was tormented with the misplaced belief that, in God's eyes, divorce was unforgivable.

It's hard to admit to being divorced. I don't believe in divorce! It's wrong! It can't be justified. It's scandalous in the eyes of God's community—the church. You will be punished! Ostracized! God hates it (and thus hates you!) God can never use you again. And the biggie: THE BIBLE SAYS (... said ominously with the read-between-the-lines-worst-case-scenario left hanging in the air).

Anne has talked about how the Amish and Mennonite sects are known for shunning members for infringements of their strict rules. It's not just the Amish and Mennonites. I know shunning. In the independent, fundamentalist, Bible-believing church where I grew up—now a vibrant and positive community of believers—divorced people were negated and disenfranchised, whispered about, and shunned. Somehow, in spite of that, there were a number of dear people who came Sunday after Sunday, head hung low, humbly trying to find a place in the otherwise loving community of believers.

A family friend of ours, a learned Bible scholar, teacher, and savvy businessman, was, with one fell swoop, relieved of his church duties when his divorce was made known.

Why did he get the divorce? His cantankerous wife was beating him up with her crutch, for heaven's sake! This was a fact not lost on my young teen psyche. I wondered: Is divorce really the unpardonable sin?

Another scenario vivid in my mind is the lady who didn't seem to have a proper name. "That divorced woman" was what she was called. To this day, just thinking of her brings tears to my eyes. She was so beaten up by shame that she would regularly get into a tub filled with tepid water and each time she soaked she would increase the temperature of the water. Finally, as a last-ditch effort in doing penance for her sin, she began to boil the water. With pot after pot of scalding water, she performed her ultimate sacrament.

Blistered beyond repair, shedding great sheets of skin like a molting animal, they took her away to a mental hospital, never to be heard from again.

"That's what sin does to you," some said.

There were many years I would have described my marriage as great, even ideal. The breakdown of my marriage—the verbal, emotional, and spiritual abuse—happened in tiny increments and although I didn't realize it then, it was synonymous with my husband's spiral into prescription drugs and pornography. My spirit shattered into a million pieces the day he—the man I'd loved for so many years—assaulted me.

As a self-proclaimed humorist, I had written 15 books and was a speaker on the national circuit. I spoke about surviving what I called "the craziness of life" and coming out better than before. I had presented myself as the person with all the answers. Now I had no answers. I even questioned my sanity.

When the police officer who came to my aid after my assault asked if I was going to press charges, I remembered the many women who had fallen into my arms after a speaking engagement to pour out their stories of abuse and whose spiritual leaders had urged them to let it go.

"Don't embarrass yourself and the church," they said. "Forgive, forgive, FORGIVE!"

In other words, sweep it under the rug so we don't have to deal with it.

I pressed charges ... for them and for me.

I describe my life at that time as being in the pit of hell. My life truly fell apart—not just the divorce, but my precious daughter died, at Christmas no less. I lost my voice from the trauma and, with that, the disappearance of any semblance of financial security, the home I loved, and much more. I was back to square minus-four in more ways than I can count.

Discovering the Imprecatory Psalms was my first step to spiritual sanity. These are the honest, often angry, Psalms. The ones we pretty much ignored, at least in my religious history, in favor of "A soft answer turns away wrath" and all that. These are the curses that invoke evil, that call down punishment on one's enemy. The ones that admit to hopelessness: "I sink in deep mire, where there is no foothold."(ESV)

If only you could see the notes in the margins of my Bible! Those hateful Psalms resonated with me in my anger and despair. Like David (or whoever it was who wrote Psalms—I'm no theologian), I was angrier than a rabid Doberman chasing the mailman. And I was bone-tired. "I am weary with my crying out. My throat is parched. My eyes grow dim with waiting for my God." And right there, in the margins of my Bible, next to that particular verse in Psalms 69, SOMEONE wrote DAMMIT! I wasn't even allowed to say a word like that, but those words from Scripture gave me permission to get mad and to express that anger. That anger was never at God (although most do get angry at God) but at the situation, at my husband, and at the misplaced teachings of the churches of our upbringings.

We were bombarded with the notion of God's wrath—if not wrath, then His displeasure. We were held captive by warnings of "unpardonable" sins. WE WERE FILTHY RAGS, for heaven's sake! Our churches used Scripture (sometimes out of context) to control us and manipulate our thinking.

I often say, "Had my husband—the son of a hard-core fundamentalist preacher—known as much about God's love as he did about sin, he would have lived a different life."

After my angry streak, I began to feel as though I was falling through the air with no parachute. I could only gasp the word "help," and it was my helplessness that seduced me into the arms of a loving God. It felt like falling into a humongous pile of goose down comforters and pillows ... and ... clouds maybe. Since then, and to this day, it's the goodness of God that informs my life.

Childhood brain-washing still rears its ugly head at times, but the overpowering truth is this: I am so loved and so treasured by the God of the universe.

*I can't bear the thought of disappointing Him. I'm
safe and protected ... and loved beyond measure. I
live now in the holiest of places: his arms!*

Stories like Sue's are too common, especially since we know at least one-third of the women sitting in churches every week are survivors of abuse. I can't count the number of people who have come to me with stories they did not feel safe to share in their churches. They feared being shunned, blamed, or ignored. Some continued to put themselves in harm's way, staying with abusive spouses, convinced that no one would believe them or understand if they left when churches should be the first place where people feel safe enough to tell the truth. Church communities fall prey to the same lies that keep victims silent when leaders ignore, minimize, or cover up reports of abuse in the interest of protecting a church's untarnished image.

Silencing victims is dangerous and far-reaching. It only serves to protect predators.

And protecting predators only serves to silence the abused.

CHAPTER 7
The Generational Impact of Shame

*"Unlike guilt, which is the feeling of
doing something wrong,
shame is the feeling of being something wrong."*
Marilyn J. Sorensen

Throughout my years growing up, no one talked about shame. Every human since the Garden of Eden has likely experienced shame at some level. I could always feel shame's presence but was never given a name for that feeling. When I was a young woman, if you asked me what shame had to do with me, I would have told you that Jesus covered my shame when he died on the cross and I was no longer a slave to it. But the truth is, I *was* a slave to shame because I did not know how to dismantle the lies I believed about myself.

Shame is commonly confused with guilt, but the differences are profound.

> **Guilt is the realization that I have**
> ***done* something wrong.**
> **Shame assumes there is something**
> **wrong with *me*.**

Like a subliminal script, constantly playing in the background of our minds, shame tells us untrue stories about ourselves. Shame is far more destructive than guilt. The way it intertwines our pain with our identity actually alters the chemistry of our brains over time, in the same way that trauma does. Shame convinced me that I was unworthy of the life I desired. It convinced me that I was incapable of lasting relationships. Shame made me believe that I was to blame for anything that went wrong in my family's lives and for my kids' decisions.

Shame tells us we deserve the pain we experience, that we do not deserve what we need and long for because there is something fundamentally wrong with us.

Only when we begin to understand the lies we believe are we able to dismantle the foundation of shame on which abuse and addiction are built. Shame drives everything in toxic relationships. It drove wedges into every important relationship in my life—before, during, and after the abusive relationship with Pastor. I didn't understand how messages of shame silently wormed their way into my very identity. And there is nothing more isolating than shame. Its very nature creates disconnection. I was convinced that if my secrets got out, Jonas would leave me forever, my family would disown me, and I would lose everything. If that indeed happened, my shame would have only been further reinforced and the disconnection from my family would have destroyed me.

That's what shame does. When it goes unaddressed, it destroys.

I remember feeling as if a track in my mind just kept repeating the same thoughts over and over again, thoughts made of the lies I believed that kept me stuck in that cycle. Not until I searched all the way back to the trauma of Angie's death could I begin to dismantle the lies that originally set me on this destructive path. I had to identify the "why" of my pain.

In order to break the shame cycle, you have to understand what's true and what isn't. Trying over and over again to simply numb pain and soothe shame doesn't work. Shame is too much to bear. Our bodies and minds were not created to carry it. If we don't find healing, the shame finds a way out and spills over onto the people around us.

My shame spilled over onto Jonas. I blamed him for making me feel isolated, even though I could never effectively get rid of shame by transferring it to others. By that method, it only multiplies, keeping the cycle going. Until I knew how to identify its destructive patterns, it seemed like a self-fulfilling prophecy. The truth is, Jonas was not the reason I felt isolated. My isolation took root long before I even met him. Growing up, I already felt disconnected and excluded. I look back and see how shame even shaped the way I assumed God felt about me. It warped my understanding, reducing God to a harsh scorekeeper. I believed that if I didn't live a life that was pleasing to Him or if I broke the rules of the church, He would be displeased, and I would reap what I sowed. I thought I was doing everything right, so I couldn't fathom what I did to deserve losing my daughter.

Shame's self-sabotaging lies convinced me that I did not deserve the one thing I ever wanted in life: a happy family. And my own perceived lack of worth was passed along to my living daughters in so many subtle ways. During the formational years of their lives, when they most needed to know they were safe and worthy of love, I knew of no other way to function. I could not pass on truths about their own value that I didn't believe myself.

I now see with more clarity. I see that I could never have experienced wholeness as long as I was under the vice grip of shame. I would always find someone or something to blame for my misery as long as the lies I believed went unaddressed. Of course, I still wish Angie was with me today but blaming God or myself only kept me trapped in that cycle of pain, blame, and shame. And as long as that cycle continued, I was in the way of my own healing. I now have a very different understanding of the way God interacts with us. Now I believe that when I hurt, He weeps with me.

Shame is such a deeply painful emotion. It projects onto the people around us unless truth is allowed to shine through the lies and heal our broken places. This pastor was a predator who brought pain into the lives of so many people for his own sick pleasure. Still, shame convinced me I could do nothing and tell no one. It would take decades to even be able to say his name out loud. My sisters and I only referred to him as "the beast" until very recently. I was constantly held back by the beliefs that I would never be fully loved, fully forgiven, or fully trusted if word ever got out about my relationship with him. While I lived under this umbrella of shame, I never considered the potential this predator had to harm others. His capacity for evil did not stop with us.

I never imagined my story could get any worse, until it did. After my sisters and I broke our silence about our abuse, I was hit with the final bombshell 15 years later.

He had preyed on LaWonna, too.

LaWonna was only four years old when she began carrying her own secret. After her marriage came to an end, she was trying to find healing and asked me to come with her to a counseling appointment, which made me happy because I wanted healing for my whole family. During that appointment, she shared the worst news I could have ever heard, recalling how Pastor molested her repeatedly for years.

I still shudder to imagine how alone she would have felt as a defenseless child and how this horror had silently shaped her view of the world, of herself, of God, and of the church. She had been through so much already and was navigating our difficult family story as a defenseless child while bearing this horrible secret. I was devastated and angrier than I can possibly describe. I went home and collapsed into Jonas's arms, weeping. I was angry at myself, at the pastor, and at God.

I didn't pray audibly for three years after that day. I couldn't. Every time I started to pray audibly, I felt like I would choke. The realization hit hard that shame had kept me silent. My silence allowed this beast to continue finding more victims ... not nameless victims, but children ... and not nameless children, but my own LaWonna.

By the time LaWonna was able to verbalize what he did to her at that counseling appointment, two decades had passed. We took steps to see if charges could be filed for the crime committed against her, but Pennsylvania state laws were not working in our favor at that time, and we were ultimately not able to meet the burden of proof 20 years later. It was hard to let that go. Speaking out and seeking justice wouldn't change what he did, but it would have allowed LaWonna the opportunity to break her silence, take back her voice, and finally force him to face consequences.

LaVale, who was born during my years of abuse, bore scars of her own as she grew up. She's very perceptive. Somehow, she knew there were secrets the family wasn't telling her. I didn't want her to feel like an outsider in her own family as the only one who wasn't filled in on this difficult part of our life. So, when she was 14 I tried to tell her the story. I did not yet fully understand myself how different an affair is from the abuse I experienced, and I was not able to verbalize the distinction to LaVale the first time I shared my past with her. As far as she knew, I was unfaithful to her dad and was lying to cover it up.

When I assured LaVale that Jonas is, without question, her father, she was convinced I was lying, even when I explained that the sexual abuse began after I became pregnant with her. I had hoped telling her the truth would build trust between us, but instead it destroyed her trust in me. The relationship between us changed that day. I was tired of the lies but telling the truth was costly.

And there went shame, rearing its ugly head again. The pain of my story penetrated LaVale's heart and shame became part of her identity. I was powerless to reverse the cycle of shame in my daughters' lives, which became my great sorrow.

Just like when I was growing up, shame and secrets become woven again so tightly into the fabric of our lives that healing and clarity seemed impossible. And my family's story is not nearly as unique as you might imagine. The shame cycle is at play everywhere you turn, spreading like wildfire through marriages, families, communities, and churches.

If left unhealed, that cycle repeats for generations.

Truly, the bonds of shame have spared no one in my family. As long as I lived as a victim in the cycle of shame, I couldn't change the ending of my story. Blaming others, complaining about all that "happened to me," and off-loading my shame onto people I cared about kept me from taking any responsibility for hurting others. I felt trapped in a relationship that I felt powerless to end and my eventual journey toward healing was slow and full of setbacks. I am eternally grateful for the people who eventually came along and helped me understand that my story does not have to end in shame.

If you find yourself stuck in the cycle of shame, your story does not have to end there either, dear reader. And neither did the story of my friend, Kim. She was raised very differently than I was, and her story is unique, yet the generational impact of shame wreaked havoc in her story, too.

I grew up with an abusive, alcoholic father. He and my mom did not raise my younger sister and me in church, so we didn't know anything about God. As a little girl, I had no idea it wasn't normal for dads to be passed out at the kitchen table. I didn't know other girls' fathers didn't hit them for no reason other than they were standing too close. I thought all little girls were awakened at 2:00 AM by their fathers' fury and scared to death of whatever was going to happen next. I thought the way my dad treated my sister and I was normal.

The years from kindergarten through third grade were extremely difficult for me at school. I was a bully to the other kids. My teachers didn't know what to do and neither did my mom, but she put me in counseling.

By the time I reached fourth grade, I started standing up for myself, my sister, and my mom. I was very angry with my dad and angry that he could not see what the alcohol was doing to him and our family. I was angry at my mom for not standing up to him and protecting us. He would promise over and over again that he would stop drinking.

He never did.

By about age 13, I was done with my dad and his lies. I was tired of competing with the alcohol. I realized what he was doing to us was abuse and I learned not to cover for him. In fact, I learned how to blame everything that went wrong in my life on my dad. I would go to his hiding spots and pour out his liquor. My fear had turned into anger ... I almost dared him to scare me again.

Up until this time, the only positive father figure I had in my life was my grandfather. I adored him. When he went into the hospital and was not expected to live, I would make deals with God to keep my grandfather alive. And when he died, I was furious at God, too.

I always hated my dad for continually choosing alcohol over us. I hated that he thought he could control us and get us to do what he wanted, yet he could not control himself with alcohol.

I could never stand for my dad to touch me. I hated when he hugged me, and I always figured it was because of the hate I had for him from the physical and mental abuse.

But then around 20 years old, I started having flashbacks of being sexually abused by my dad. The details took time to resurface and my mind protected me from some of the details because I was so young. My sister also remembered being sexually abused. I believe the years when my sexual abuse happened were from five years of age to around eight, which makes a lot of sense when I look back at how difficult those years were for me. By the time I reached fourth grade, he had moved on to my younger sister, Kelley.

I spent the next several years running as I tried to process these memories, questioning everything and putting the pieces together. Why would a father who loves his little girls ever do something so horrible to them? Where was my mom? Why didn't I tell anyone? Was it my fault?

I can remember being a scared little girl, lying in bed and just praying that he would pass by my door. I remember how relieved I would feel when his footsteps stopped at my sister's door. I didn't understand what that meant until recently. I always thought I had protected her and was devastated to think that I failed her at the most important time.

As time went on, I dated the wrong guys, looking for a love that I thought they could give me. But over and over, I found myself competing with alcohol or drugs. Eventually, alcohol became my drug of choice as well. Then I dated a guy who enjoyed alcohol and cocaine and that's when my journey with drugs began.

By that time, my parents were divorced, and my sister and I did not have much contact with our father. I was grateful that, no matter what, I always had my mom and Kelley.

But on December 3, 1995, my sister was hit by a car and killed.

I was devastated. She died on a Sunday and the Friday before she died she called me at work and was so excited. She had just come from a counseling appointment and told me, "I finally figured it out. I want to become a survivor, NOT a victim!"

After she died, I felt like those words were her final gift to me. I just didn't know what to do with them. I blamed my dad for Kelley dying and couldn't deal with the pain. I couldn't deal with my mom. I did not know where I fit into this world anymore. I felt like nobody wanted me.

One night, about two months after Kelley died, I had a dream in which she told me, "Open up your heart and let God in ..."

I thought, "Yeah right."

At this point, because of that dream, I really started to think about my life. I decided to break up with my boyfriend and said "no more" to drugs and alcohol. I made a list of what I was looking for in a man:

- ✦ *No addictions*
- ✦ *A man who had nothing for me to compete with*
- ✦ *Someone who loved me for ME*

For the first time in my life I started to take responsibility for my actions and choices and stopped blaming everyone else for the way I was feeling. I started to process the gift from my sister; I began my journey as a survivor and not as a victim.

Only three months after I began that journey, I met Dennis, who was everything I hoped for and more. He told me that if our relationship was going to work, we had to put God in the middle of it.

"Oh great, the God thing again," I thought.

I struggled to accept my Heavenly Father because of all I endured from my earthly father. If I was not worthy enough for my earthly father to love me and protect me, why would God, my Heavenly Father?

- ✦ **All I ever wanted from my dad was ...** *Love, acceptance, an apology ... I wanted him to want me as much as he wanted his alcohol.*

- ✦ **All I got from my dad was ...** *Rejection, pain, disappointment ... the feeling that I was unworthy of his love.*

- ✦ **Growing up I felt ...** *Used, worthless, unimportant, embarrassed, guilty, controlled, afraid, ashamed, defenseless, insecure, and abandoned.*

I was blessed to have friends who showed me what my Heavenly father was offering me. They showed me that He has always been there with me—I just never accepted Him. My Heavenly father offers me grace, unconditional love, forgiveness, and redemption. He rescued me. My Heavenly father loves me all of the time, even when I screw up.

When we try to lead ourselves, we get lost and end up worshipping the wrong things. Even if my earthly father let me down, my Heavenly Father was there to lift me up. Because of His love, I now choose:

✦ *Not to be the victim anymore, but a survivor*
✦ *To take responsibility for my own actions and choices*
✦ *To let go of trying to control everything*
✦ *To talk and share my story*
✦ *To be thankful for the people who have been placed on my path*

Today, I am married to Dennis, who is an awesome husband. We have three wonderful kids and I am happy to be me.

Losing my sister was the worst thing that ever happened to me, yet it was also the best because of what I learned as I healed. I know now that there is always a reason for our pain and struggles, and He always brings purpose out of our pain.

CHAPTER 8

A New View of Confession

"You own everything that happened to you.
Tell your stories.
If people wanted you to write warmly about them,
they should've behaved better."
Anne Lamott

My story includes loss and abuse, but trauma and pain come in many forms. Trauma can come in the form of a life-changing diagnosis, a divorce, an accident, a financial disaster, a loss, perils of war, and other catastrophic events. But everyone's story of pain has one thing in common: it changes them.

Pain and trauma create a new reality. For me, the trauma of abuse resulted in an incredibly dysfunctional life that took me far from where I wanted to be in life … and far, far away from the person I wanted to be. So much so that I gave up on deciding how the rest of my life would go. I became an unhappy spectator in my own life, whining and complaining about all the things done to me. I believed I was powerless to participate in my own life story. I *believed* I had no voice in my own life story; therefore, I didn't.

Before I could reconnect with myself, I had to free myself from my prison of lies and secrets. I had to interact with the truth in ways I had never known.

What I would discover along my road toward healing is that owning the whole truth of my story would mean redefining everything I knew about confession. For many, confession is intertwined with guilt, shame, and punishment when, really, confession simply means breaking our silence. It's about freedom, and it's about getting back into the driver's seat of our own stories.

Trauma and abuse survivors do not need to apologize for our pain, but we do need to express *everything* that happened and own the entire truth of it.

For me, confession included owning the dysfunctional way I was interacting with everyone in my life. It meant admitting to the fear that paralyzed me and confessing the lies I believed, the ones that ended up derailing my life. I love the Psalm that says, "So I remained utterly silent, not even saying anything good. But my anguish increased; my heart grew hot within me. While I meditated, the fire burned; then I spoke with my tongue!" (Psalm 39:2-3 NIV)

Five years into the abuse, it is safe to say that my heart had grown hot within me. In fact, I felt as if the framework of my soul was about to snap.

At that time, Jonas took a job near Troup, Texas, and we moved our family. My sisters and their families also moved to a nearby town. But our pain followed us there, both figuratively and literally.

Within a few months, Pastor had moved his family to town too. He was originally from that area, so he simply reestablished contact and proceeded to start a church there, and he picked up where he left off with us. I kept hoping to find a way out without having to reveal the ugly truth. After five years of trying to deny the truth of my story, I felt completely hijacked by it. Confession was incremental for me … It all started with one little truth.

———•◦•———

I vividly remember driving down Troup highway, between Jacksonville and Troup, Texas, in a 1966 Chevelle convertible Jonas had restored. As I drove, I was actively searching the side of the highway for places where I could drive off the road and end it all. Around that same time, when the misery seemed impossible to bear alone, my phone rang. It was my brother, Chub, calling just to see if I was okay. I was surprised by his concern. By that time, I weighed only 92 pounds, was deeply depressed, and seriously contemplating suicide, yet I had no idea anyone would suspect that I was struggling. I thought I was pulling it off without a trace.

In reply to Chub's question, I mustered up the most upbeat tone I could force, "I'm fine! Why do you ask?"

"I just had you on my mind," he said. I could hear the genuine concern in his voice. He told me he had been praying for me and just felt like he needed to call and check on me.

I couldn't speak. I didn't want to lie, but I couldn't bear to say out loud what was really wrong.

Then he asked again, "Are you *sure* you're okay?"

After a long silence, I uttered, "No, I'm not okay, but please don't ask me what's wrong."

He paused, then asked, "Does it have anything to do with the pastor?"

As any secret brings along heightened sensitivity, his guess convinced me in that moment that he knew everything. I told him again that I couldn't talk about what was wrong. Much to my relief, he didn't press any further and was gracious and reassuring. I look back on that phone conversation with Chub as the first truth, however small, I was able to tell after years of hiding behind my lies. I didn't tell him everything, but I did experience my first authentic moment in years when I admitted that I wasn't okay, and I'll never forget the relief that came from not being the only person carrying the full weight of my pain anymore. That first truth gave me a tiny glimpse of hope.

I had been so afraid that if I told anyone in my family I wasn't okay, I would disappoint them. Not knowing how the trauma had changed me or that shame was distorting my view of reality, I constantly worried about what people would think if they knew all the secrets I was carrying. I was so disconnected from myself, so uninformed about trauma, that I didn't even have the words to explain what was wrong.

On a Saturday night several months later, I woke up in the middle of the night with all kinds of thoughts spinning around my head, which happened often in the midst of my slow confession. In that moment, I had an overwhelming longing to be close to my sisters again.

When I walked into church from the back the next morning, I saw an open seat next to Fi. And when I sat down, she put her arm around my shoulder. I felt a warmth from her that I hadn't felt in a long time. That small sign of support meant so much to me and made me feel connected to her again.

After church, Fi suggested that we meet for coffee in the morning.

"Are you sure? Will you be home?" I asked. By that time, I somehow knew Mondays were one of the days when Pastor usually met her. I was afraid she wouldn't be there when I set out the next day, but she was waiting for me when I arrived.

On that Monday morning, sitting at Fi's kitchen table having coffee, we spoke of our relationships with the pastor for the very first time.

Fi told me she wasn't seeing him anymore. She knew I was seeing him too, so I confided in her and told her I didn't know what to do. Fi assured me she would help me get out. That morning with Fi was my second confession. Fi knew the truth and was still willing to support me. That conversation gave me another ounce of courage and resolve to find a way to free myself from his control. I had tried to leave him multiple times, only to be manipulated into staying. But, at last, after six long years of abuse, Fi's support helped me end the relationship once and for all.

Those first couple of truths I told removed a few bricks from the walls of my isolation, letting a little more light in with each one. The relief I felt was profound and each one gave me courage to take yet another step.

Eventually, the time came when I decided it was time to pick up the phone and tell Pastor's wife about the relationship. With no understanding of abuse at that point, I took full responsibility and confessed to an affair. I thought if I told this one additional truth (or what I thought was the truth), I could find relief for my guilt and finally put this nightmare behind me. I just wanted to be able to move on with my life.

But the pastor's wife asked the one question that would change everything for me.

She asked if I had told Jonas.

At that moment, I knew I had no choice but to make the one confession that terrified me the most. I didn't want Jonas to hear this news from anyone but me, even though I was sure it would mark the end of our marriage.

My heart was pounding as I made the two-mile drive to Jonas's shop. Our relationship was struggling long before this day, so there was no reason to believe we would—or even could—survive a confession of this magnitude. I summoned all the courage I had to tell Jonas. When I got to his shop, I walked up to him and immediately told him what I had come to say—short and to the point.

I looked in his eyes and said, "Hon, you've heard about Pastor and the women. Well, I'm one of those women. I'm sorry. And I'm a very sorry person."

Jonas didn't say a word. The look on his face said it all. Without another word, I walked back out to my truck and headed for work.

At the time, I was working at a steak house down the road from his shop and on that particular day, I was supposed to work from 11:00 AM until 2:00 PM. The entire three hours I ran all the scenarios through my mind. I called his shop several times during my shift, but he didn't pick up the phone, and my thoughts continued to race all afternoon. When I finally got home from work, he wasn't there. The longer I went without hearing from him, the more convinced I became that he would tell me to leave when he got home. I was pacing the floors in our home and, every few minutes, I would pull back the curtains of the picture window in our living room to see if he was coming. Finally, his truck pulled into the driveway.

For seven years, I'd feared this day. All those years dreading what the truth would mean had led up to this moment.

He walked into the kitchen and said, "Hon, we need to talk."

I burst out, "About what?" Of course, I knew "what" but *that* was my lifelong pattern ... to avoid the things that most needed to be said. Only this time, I couldn't avoid them anymore.

He said that we needed to talk once the girls were tucked in for the night. I can hardly remember anything that happened during the next few excruciating hours until the girls went to bed. My assumption was that the conversation he wanted was how to proceed with a separation and divorce.

Hours later, after the girls were settled into bed, we stood in the kitchen and I braced myself for his wrath. Jonas spoke first.

"I knew you were unhappy, but I thought it was because of Angie's death. I do want you to be happy," he said.

He wants me to be happy?

I couldn't believe he wasn't going to take this opportunity to criticize me. If he had shamed me for telling the truth, I would have walked out the door. I couldn't take any more guilt than I already felt.

But he went on to say, "I want you to promise me something ..."

I didn't want to trust myself to make a promise and started crying, "I don't know if I can promise anything."

Then he started to cry, too as he said, "Promise me you won't leave a note on the dresser in the middle of the night. If you decide to go, I want to help you. I'll even help you find a place and pack your bags. But please take the girls with you. They need their mother. If you need to leave, we'll plan it together."

By this time, he was sobbing.

I promised him, through my own sobs, that I would not leave in the night and that I would remain in the girls' life. I felt a spark of hope deep in my soul that said this wasn't the end for us. I hadn't considered the possibility that he would forgive me and never dared to dream he would want to remain in this marriage. The raw vulnerability between us was completely new territory for me. It felt strange and uncomfortable, yet I felt more connected to Jonas—and to myself. I see now how the confessions that led me to that moment had already begun to shape me and launch me into an entirely new way of life as everything I was afraid of happening just didn't happen.

I was ready for Jonas to berate me, leave me, condemn me, or any number of other possible negative responses.

But I was unprepared for him to forgive me.

We had been silently coexisting for so long, and this conversation was one I never imagined having with Jonas. Until that moment, I never imagined that confessing could offer me hope. That confession was the pivotal moment in my journey toward peace and healing. When Jonas told me the truth about myself—that the girls needed their mother—I was completely overwhelmed. He gave me hope for myself and for my family. Honestly, I didn't have any idea how that would play out or look down the road. In that moment, I felt deep respect and gratitude for my husband.

Even though telling Jonas the truth was terribly difficult, that conversation gave me more hope than I had felt in years. With one conversation, Jonas demonstrated what safe relationships need most, and certainly what *I* needed.

He showed me that I *can* talk,
I *can* trust, and I *can* feel.

I heard stories about Jesus all my life, and my sisters and I spent years singing about Him and serving in church, but I'd never felt the love of Jesus more powerfully than I did through Jonas during my confession.

And so, our recovery began.

A few days later, I remember being in the bathroom and Jonas was in the bedroom, and I asked him if we could really make this work or if we were going to have to get a divorce. As soon as I said that, Jonas fell to the floor and groaned a terrible groan, unlike anything I had ever heard from him. He never yelled or cursed at me, but this response was more of an outcry, as if the weight of everything finally made him crumble into a pile there on the floor of our room.

Through groans and sobs, he said, "Don't ever use the word divorce in this home."

Just like that, I could no longer avoid taking responsibility for my life, my choices, and my family. I had to begin choosing how I would respond to my pain instead of being consumed by it. I began to fight for my life and for my family. I had to make changes and do whatever I had to do to make them stick. One of the biggest realizations was when I became aware that I needed to put better things in my mind. I also decided not to go places without Jonas. We would do this together. I didn't trust myself and I was still afraid of our pastor. I feared that he might try to harm me or my family. Even still, with all those changes, there were moments when I felt like running away from it all.

But I could never have predicted the positive outcomes of my confession. Realizing that we don't have to shoulder the burden of our brokenness alone brings more relief than anyone can possibly predict in those moments of running all the messy scenarios through our minds.One of the most terrifying things about confession is the fear of what people will think if we confess the things we've done, what happened to us, or how we are feeling. Up until that time, every ounce of my energy was spent maintaining my image. I was obsessed with what people thought of me. Yet, having the courage to be authentic was empowering beyond belief, and letting others see that was not as devastating as I thought it would be.

The truth I had spent years avoiding turned out to be the very thing that created connection again in my life. I shared with Jonas that I was afraid to go to church, that I was worried word was getting around and what people must think of me. Sharing my fears with him allowed him to carry the burden with me.

He assured me again and again, "You don't have to do this alone. You don't have to defend the truth. You don't have to do anything. I will do this *with* you."

In addition, my confession led me to new discoveries about what had actually happened to me and my sisters. We all began to see the enormity of the pain this abuser caused and how far he was willing to go to deceive, control, and use his influence for evil. His web of lies was tangled and far-reaching beyond our imaginations.

Confession lets people in. It allows light to flood the darkness of secrets, so we can see clearly.

Six years after the abuse began, I went to a counselor with Jonas. I didn't want to go, but I knew if our marriage was going to survive that I needed to go. I didn't know how to talk about the past few years, and I was sick and tired of being sick and tired. But I still didn't know how to live any other way. I didn't even have the words to explain how I was feeling.

Perhaps the trauma kept me from being able to trust a counselor after being vulnerable with my pastor years earlier went so terribly wrong. The counselor we saw tried several different ways of helping me process all that was going on inside my heart and mind, but I just wouldn't open up. I didn't want to feel weak.

I had spent too many years pretending to be strong.

Finally, fresh out of ideas, our counselor asked me at the end of our third appointment to make a list of 10 things I liked about myself and bring it to my next appointment. I tried to think of something, but a week later, I still couldn't come up with a single thing I liked about myself.

After that, our counselor started to open up and shared his own struggles. He was vulnerable, and I realized that he too had experienced hard things in his life. In a last-ditch attempt to get me to open up, he finally he asked me the right question, "What are the three biggest disappointments in your life?"

I knew that answer right away, and it opened a flood of emotion.

I confessed that I was disappointed with Angie's death, Jonas's silence, and the constant rejection I received (at great cost) from my perpetrator and my sisters during the previous few years.

From that moment on, after acknowledging my three disappointments, my three vulnerabilities, I was able to be honest and open during our sessions. Each truth, each confession, each authentic reaction was one more step in the direction of freedom.

CHAPTER 9

The Power of Telling the Truth

"When we can talk about our feelings, they become less overwhelming, less upsetting, and less scary. The people we trust with that important talk can help us know that we are not alone."
Fred Rogers

The truth is powerful.

As the truth began to transform my thoughts, my behaviors began to change as well ... and slowly, things around me began to change. Freedom becomes a possibility when the truth is finally known.

But that doesn't make it easy to tell.

It wasn't until *after* I started telling the truth that I truly believed it could set me free. I can honestly say that, if Jonas had not responded graciously, or my family had not been supportive, or other pastors had not stepped in and confronted our abuser, I *would still* be glad I told the truth. Looking back, there were three different kinds of confessions that gradually led me out of the dark. As I've said, confessing and being able to tell the truth was all incremental for me.

Bedside confessions were the first method I found to express what was buried deep inside me. Bedside prayers were safe. I knew I could trust Jesus and that my secret was safe with Him. So, on my knees in silent prayer is where I began my inward journey toward healing. Even though I couldn't always outwardly express the things I needed to say, I could at least ask God for help and forgiveness. But prayer alone couldn't lighten the load I felt.

Journaling was my second type of confession. I didn't think I could do it at first. It started when my counselor asked me to write down how I was feeling. I really didn't have any idea how to do that, but he told me to just start writing. I started scribbling out whatever I was feeling onto a yellow legal pad and quickly found that I couldn't stop writing. I would fill the front and back of nine or 10 pages of that legal pad in one sitting. And as I read what I had written, I couldn't believe all the feelings inside me.

Writing helped me, but it was certainly riskier than praying, and I worried that someone might see what I had written. Journaling is very different from keeping a diary. My mother kept a diary of what she did each day for most of her adult life. You could look up any date and find the daily tasks she completed, who came to visit, and so forth. But a journal is specifically focused on what's happening inside you—feelings, memories, reflections, and other things you might not be ready to admit to another person.

When I wasn't sure who to talk to or what to do next, I could fill page after page with all the things I needed to get out. I still love to journal even today. Documenting moments and experiences as they are happening remains a valuable part of processing daily life. But even journaling the truth couldn't change the trajectory of my life without the last piece of my confession.

The third type of confession—what I call "one to another"—was the piece that ultimately helped me move to a new place emotionally, spiritually, and physically by allowing me to share my journey of pain. This type of confession broke all the internal barriers that let me keep feeding on lies.

But this truth-telling had to be ongoing, or I would begin to slip backwards.

As I began to free myself from the secrets of my past, I could see the world more clearly. I saw my older sister, Becky, still trapped by the deception of it all. Our pastor had brainwashed her for so long that I worried she wouldn't find a way out. I knew the truth would feel hurtful to her; yet, I felt a sense of urgency about telling her.

One Sunday night, I could hardly sleep as I felt the courage building inside me to finally talk to her. The wall between us had grown impenetrable over the years. I was afraid she would reject me and then whatever was left of our relationship would be gone.

But the next morning, as I pulled up to the school to drop my kids off, I saw Becky's car ahead. After my kids got out, I passed by her car, rolled down my window, and told her that I needed to talk to her and I would wait.

Becky knew I had been in a relationship with our pastor too, and she knew I had left him. But we'd never spoken a word about it. I was terrified to confront my sister about this and it took all my courage to talk to her that day.

When she drove up next to my car, we talked through our open car windows. In some way, that felt safe. It provided the buffer that I needed in that moment since I couldn't think about anything other than what I had to say.

I jumped right in, saying, "Beck! He doesn't love you! He's lying to you …"

I could immediately see from the look on her face that she didn't believe me. I'm sure it was terrifying for her to imagine ever trying to break free from his grip. I had heard all his lies myself and I understood her fear and disbelief in that moment. I rattled off the name of someone else he was seeing and suggested that Becky call the woman and ask her if she didn't believe me. She sped off, clearly agitated.

But soon after that conversation, she was able to see clearly enough to escape his abuse after 10 long and exhausting years.

For the first time since the abuse began, the truth not only set me free, but also my sisters. We, along with our husbands, became a lifeline for each other. We spent a lot of time with each other over the months that followed, talking for hours about everything we had experienced—laughing, crying, expressing all the emotions we had bottled up for so many years. I had my sisters back in my life, and this time we had a deeper connection than ever before. What many people find in a support group, we found in each other. We experienced so much healing together as we processed our experiences.

There were no longer secrets between us.

During so many of those conversations, one question kept coming up: "How can we stop him?"

We were afraid of him, and with good reason. After the depths of evil we had witnessed, we knew he was capable of hurting us or our family members. He told me more than once that he would haunt me for the rest of my life. While we knew he was an evil man, none of us understood that abuse was a crime or that he was a predator. We had been taught not to question authority and the highest authority we knew was our denominational leaders. My sisters and our families concluded that we needed to start there—with our denomination's leaders.

Although it took some time, we established contact with the council of pastors responsible for overseeing our network of churches. After many months of communication, spearheaded by our husbands, a date was set for the meeting where we could share with our denomination's authorities the hell on earth we, and many others, had endured.

When the day came for us to face the council, we were scared to death. We knew how important it would be to tell the truth to the only people we knew who could stop him.

Pastor was supposed to attend that meeting but never showed up. We were relieved to have an opportunity to be totally honest with the council. Once we shared our stories, the council asked each of us to provide them with a detailed description of times and places where we met him, how many encounters we had, and many other embarrassing details in order to verify our stories. Afterwards, a second meeting was scheduled and, once again, our pastor was invited. And, once again, he was not present when the meeting began.

About 15 minutes into that second meeting, we heard a knock on the door. It was Pastor, who approached the table where the council was seated and presented a letter from his wife before saying anything else. We don't know what the letter said, but the man leading the council only glanced at it briefly before continuing with the meeting, stating that the letter did not pertain to the purpose of the meeting. Pastor was asked to take a seat in the back of the room where he could observe—but not control—the meeting. That was a powerful moment for us, when telling the truth finally overruled the power his lies and secrecy held over us for so many years.

That council of pastors not only believed us, but stood up to our predator in front of us and our spouses. They took away his license and assured us that he would never minister in our denomination again. They expressed their outrage and were visibly devastated that this abuse happened on their watch. Their response was redemptive to us at a time when we desperately needed support from the body of Christ. By coming to our defense, the seven leaders on that counsel renewed the hope Pastor stole from us. We fought a hard battle, but emerged victorious in the end.

We couldn't control what he did after that day, but he could no longer stop us from healing.

Knowing now what I didn't know then, one of my greatest regrets is that I was not armed with the information I needed to pursue a criminal conviction.

After a few months of quietly slipping in and out of a nearby church, we still didn't know exactly how to reengage with a church community. Eventually, Jonas and I, along with my sisters and their husbands, started attending a church in Austin, Texas. The trauma made us feel disconnected and unfit to serve. We sat together in the back as visitors, hoping not to be noticed. As the congregation sang "It Is Well With My Soul" one Sunday, I was overwhelmed with peace—peace with God, with my husband, and with my family. I watched the choir as they sang that song and pondered how much I would love to be able to sing again, and how satisfied I was that in that moment I could sit and worship. I decided that even if I never did anything else in church again, being at peace was a gift for which I was eternally grateful.

That same Sunday, a guest speaker was introduced and, much to our surprise, that speaker was one of the seven men on the pastoral counsel who'd stepped in to defend us. We had no idea he would be there and were actually worried at first. We didn't want anyone beyond our family and those seven men to know our story. Seeing him made us all want to disappear.

When he got up to speak, he pointed us out—exactly what we were afraid would happen. Not only did he recognize us, but he went on to honor us by saying that some very good friends of his were sitting in the back. He told the congregation that we were good people and he hoped we would find this church to be a loving place where we would feel welcome. Then, as part of the message that morning, all of the married couples in the church were invited to stand and renew their wedding vows.

There is no way anyone could have planned that incredible moment for us.

No one knew we would be there ... except God.

When I think about the times I thought God had forgotten me, that moment always comes to mind. After walking through the difficult process of confessing the truth of our stories, we all felt as if God was communicating with us that day, giving us a new start together. Being met with such grace gave us what we needed when the best we had hoped for was to slide into the back row without having to talk about anything that happened to us.

God did so much better than that.

There was a time we never could have imagined that kind of experience, that peace, that acceptance was possible. We were finally reaping the benefits of one-to-another confession. Truth was finally winning.

Becky recalls that, for many years after our confessions, she would become uncomfortable if she was asked to go along with a joke that stretched the truth. Even a moment of untruth, for the sake of a laugh, caused her to feel uneasy. We all felt that.

All of us, at one point, depended on lies for daily survival and never wanted to go back to that way of life, not even a little bit. Only when I remembered to harness the power of telling the truth could I continue to move forward toward healing. I learned that my long journey toward wholeness would never be wholly complete. There would always be reminders and twinges of pain but being able to talk truthfully about those things with safe people gave the reminders and the pain less power over me.

The choices I made and the moments of pain I caused could not be met with forgiveness until I confessed them. That is how I slowly inched out of darkness and secrets toward a life where I could finally taste freedom—one confession at a time. Every truth I told and every time I owned my own part in the pain, the way forward became just a little more visible.

Growing up, I thought I needed to be truthful to make *God* happy. But all along, He wanted me to tell the truth because it makes *me* happy. Walking in truth, including the beautiful and terrifying process of confession and forgiveness, leads us toward wholeness, which brings Him *and* us joy. Even when it seems impossible, truth holds the keys that unlock our prison doors.

Lies are all consuming. They occupy every open space within us, filling all the nooks and crannies with darkness, taking over our entire being. As we speak truth, we release the lies inside of us. Truth overpowers and pushes out the lie, leaving a void in its place, an empty space that needs to be filled. And every time we risk everything to tell the truth, I'm convinced that God's Spirit rushes into the void where that lie once took up space and makes us whole again.

CHAPTER 10

Do You Want to Be Well?

"Change is not what happens outside us; rather, change must first take root within us."
Ilia Delio

Growing up in church, I heard over and over again that the *lost* need to be *saved*.

What I never heard was that the *saved* need to be *healed*. When I heard stories about Jesus healing people, I didn't think they applied to me.

I had a lot to learn about healing.

◆◆◆

Knowing how trauma, grief, abuse, and shame affect our brain chemistry and physical bodies, I realized how much damage my pain would continue to cause me mentally, physically, emotionally, and spiritually. It was one particular story in John 5 that brought my attention to the long-term damage pain can have if allowed.

In the story, The Pool of Bethesda was a place in Jerusalem where crowds of sick people gathered because the water was believed to have healing properties. The area around the pool was crowded with chronically ill people—blind, lame, or paralyzed—waiting to immerse themselves in the water whenever it bubbled up. They all laid there, waiting, hoping for their chance at a miracle.

One day, Jesus came to this area and saw a man lying on a mat near the pool who had been sick for 38 years. Jesus knew he had been ill for a long time, so He asked him:

"Do you want to be well?"

Why would he ask such a thing? Wasn't the entire point of being at the pool to be well? Couldn't Jesus assume the man wanted to be healed if he had been sick for 38 years?

But the man's answer is surprising.

"I can't …"

… What?

The man goes on, "I have no one to put me into the pool when the water bubbles up. Someone else always gets there ahead of me."

Jesus told him to stand up, pick up his mat, and move to a new place. I don't know what his illness was, and I assume Jesus healed him physically in that moment for him to be able to simply stand up and move. I do know from experience that, after living as a *sick* person for 38 years, the man had to relearn how to live as a *well* person. When he could finally carry his own mat and decide where to go next, there were options he never had before.

But he had to take responsibility for getting up and moving forward into a new way of living.

At one point or another, we all find that same reality to be true in our lives. Those of us who have lived through trauma may not even know what *being well* looks like. Just like the man in the story, I waited for so long to be well, but I eventually had to get up off my knees and take responsibility for my own life. My isolation had nothing to do with anyone else. Finding fault and blaming others never improves the outcomes of our lives. But taking responsibility for our future—owning whatever part of it we need to own—is what frees us from the darkness of the past. Confessing my part allowed me to receive forgiveness from others, God, and even myself. The power of that confession helped me move forward, but that was just the beginning. I'd planted bad seeds every day for years and it took a lot of good seeds to create a better future for myself and the generations that would follow me.

The journey to freedom was much harder than I ever imagined it would be. Regardless of the pauses in my healing, after my first step into the realm of speaking truth, I never went all the way back to the dark place where I started—not once I began taking responsibility for my life.

For me, truth-telling began a new process of learning how to be well. It meant no longer blaming someone else for my pain.

Being well involves arming ourselves with better information so we can develop healthier ways of thinking. It means respecting ourselves, forming new habits, and learning to function differently on a daily basis. That can include taking advantage of helpful resources, support groups, and community programs that are designed to help people move forward into a new normal. Most people have heard that "Hurt people, hurt people." And it's true. When I was hurting, I became hurtful to others without realizing what I was doing. I had to learn how to process my pain without causing collateral damage. *Being well* meant taking responsibility and choosing to stop hurting people and break the cycle of shame. *Being well* always involves rejecting the toxic rules—*don't talk, don't trust, don't feel*—and learning how to *find* and *become* a safe person who doesn't cause pain.

For me, surrounding myself with others who also wanted to be well was such a gift. In my case, the support system of my family and a few close friends gave us all freedom to process our stories, and we made confession and storytelling part of our ongoing journey. That kind of authentic, understanding community can be lifesaving in navigating the new normal of *being well*.

For those who must grieve, *being well* involves giving ourselves permission to express our God-given feelings and walk through the stages of grief, which include: denial, anger, bargaining, depression, and, eventually, acceptance (not necessarily in that order). There is no timeline on the grieving process. Most of us experience the stages in varying degrees, moving between them many times. Grief counselors in particular can be a helpful resource for people who feel stuck and want to be well.

Being well might also include forgiving someone, starting a journal, or learning to process anger in more constructive ways. If you come to the realization that all of your emotions are being expressed as anger, it is helpful to understand that anger is often a secondary emotion fueled by fear, disappointment, or a myriad of other negative emotions—but more about anger in the next chapter.

Along the journey to *being well*, it's important to acknowledge that while you can choose to begin that journey, trauma does change your brain chemistry. There is no spiritual or emotional cure for the way trauma alters how the brain responds to stress and different individual triggers. There are, however, new and hopeful treatments for Post Traumatic Stress Disorder (PTSD) and other physical effects of trauma.

Though there is no quick fix for trauma and pain, it is possible to be well, even after living with the pain for long periods of time. And deciding to be well doesn't mean we never experience the effects of our pain again. Jonas and I will never stop grieving the loss of our daughter, but the *way* we grieve changes over time as we experience each new season of life without Angie. There is always a mixture of gratitude for her life and sorrow for our loss. Decades later, I still have moments when I break down and cry over my sweet Angie.

Sometimes I tell Jonas, "I miss our three girls today."

Often, he is feeling the same thing. That longing will never go away.

———•◦•———

Jonas and I have now been married 50 years, and both of my sisters' marriages have survived all these years as well. Considering what we all went through, that is nothing short of miraculous—but nothing about that miracle was effortless. Each morning, each of us has to choose to *be well* once again. Simply changing outward behaviors doesn't make us well. That healing has to come from the inside. We do what is ours to do and try to let go of whatever is not within our control every single day.

Gretchen is a young woman who knows, better than most, how one person's decision to become well can powerfully affect the other people in their life.

My father lives with multiple autoimmune diseases that collectively affect most systems in his body. He does not remember a time in his life when he was not battling illness and pain. Even as far back as age three, he can recall crawling towards his parents, bent over with excruciating muscular distress.

When I was still a baby, my dad was prescribed his first narcotic painkiller, the only treatment at that time for his level of pain, and he was given increasingly stronger dosages through the years. Our family story eventually revolved around his growing dependence on these painkillers.

Mom tried as hard as she could to shield me and my brother from the behaviors and chaos that inevitably come with addiction, but we knew. They surrounded us.

I see now as an adult that many of my tender years were unfairly focused on my dad instead of the carefree days of childhood. I have many happy memories of my goofy, adventurous father, but I have more of him as a sick man. As a child, you don't realize it's not your responsibility to make your parents well. My brother and I believed that somehow it was our fault that dad was "checking out" and increasingly abandoning his responsibilities.

In all his birthday and Father's Day cards, we wrote messages centered on how sick he was and how we felt so bad for him, how we'd try harder to be better kids. As I grew, so did my awareness of the dynamics that kept our family in constant turmoil.

I watched helplessly as addiction and eventually drug abuse overshadowed my dad's sweet, fun-loving personality.

My mom became my dad's caretaker, managing his medication by keeping it in a locked safe or hiding it in various places around the house. She did everything she could to protect my dad from himself. Invariably, he began desperate searches for his pills, always needing more. After all, he had real, legitimate diseases. So, the constant struggle for my family was trying to decipher between need and want, pain and addiction. We weren't equipped to manage it.

Over time, his demeanor completely changed. He became defensive, panicky, often belligerent, frequently waking us abruptly in the middle of the night demanding more medicine.

My father's addiction to and abuse of his narcotics changed the trajectory of my entire family. All of us, including my father, were very involved in our church. But no one could know the truth of what was happening behind closed doors. We lived in secrets and hid behind smoke and mirrors. My mom regularly had dreams that she was drowning; she became quiet and stoic and unemotional. My brother suppressed and escaped and poured himself into his friends and extracurriculars. I became angry and vocal, focused on being perfect and excelling in everything I could. Perfectionism became my mode of operation. I had a need to control everything because things were so out of con-

trol at home. I was desperate for the attention of my father, and the only way I knew how to get it was to be the best at whatever I did. It was exhausting.

By the time I was in junior high school, dad could no longer function in his teaching job and retired on disability. Mom took on a new job that would help provide income and benefits for our family, so whenever I wasn't attending school or doing my homework or managing my packed schedule of extracurriculars and volunteer work, I was helping care for dad and managing things at home.

Those formative years were a rollercoaster— stolen medication, overdoses, near death rescues at the hospital, excruciating drug withdrawals, and miraculous recoveries. We went through all of it, over and over again, without acknowledging my dad's secrets to anyone outside our immediate family. It was an exhausting cycle: the adrenaline and fear and sadness of the near-death experiences and then the fierce anger towards dad and his choices and what our lives had become.

It's hard to admit, but for years I hoped and prayed that dad would die. I desperately longed for my wound to heal and for my mom to find freedom from her nightmare.

But the wound kept getting ripped open, and it began to fester. The disease of bitterness and crippling anger took hold of me. My identity became victim, survivor, and angry daughter of a sick man.

I longed for a strong father figure to take care of me and my brother and my mom, but no one

*did. So, I stepped into the role of "the strong one."
I had such a tough exterior but felt so vulnerable
inside. I was still a little girl, craving the protection,
approval, and stability of my father.*

*People often congratulated me for being so
strong, for handling things so well, but inwardly
I was crying out for someone to help me. I just
wanted someone—anyone—to see my pain, to see
what I was going through, to see what was happening to my family. Those years of debilitating anger
and depression eventually impacted my relationship
with and trust of every man, while simultaneously
impacting my trust in God.*

*During my senior year of college, as our fam-
ily's secret became more and more obvious to our
community, my uncle sat down with me at a family
gathering. My anger was thinly veiled and rested
just below the surface. He asked me why I was
holding on to it. I began talking, tears streaming
down my face, and couldn't stop. I explained to him
how much I wanted someone to see my pain and to
understand how it had shaped me.*

*He then asked, "Do you want them to see a
bitter, scarred woman? Or do you want them to see
a woman who has walked through the fire and has
come out more refined and more beautiful on the
other side?"*

*His question stunned me. It shook me to my
core. I didn't want to walk through the rest of my
life smelling like the smoke of the fire that was consuming me. That day my prayers changed. Rather*

than desperately praying for people to see my pain, I began asking God to help me let go.

After college, I spent a year living in Fiji, on a deserted island with no electricity and no roads in or out. One day I was told by a missionary friend living on that island to find a big rock and carry it with me all day. At the end of the day he asked me what I thought of the experience, to which I responded, "You know, in the beginning it was a real nuisance—and so heavy! But now I barely notice it's there ... as if it has become a part of me."

"Ah," he said, "and so it is with all of the unnecessary burdens that we carry with us through life."

He challenged me to consider what emotional burdens I was carrying. And he told me, whenever I was ready, to place my rock—my burden—at the foot of a cross he had set up in the jungle nearby.

I knew immediately the burden I needed to lay down was the identity I had taken on as a victim and as the traumatized daughter of a sick man. I remember visibly shaking as I approached that cross and laid down the heavy weight I'd grown so accustomed to carrying. You would think I would've thrown that rock down with all my might and leaped for joy. Instead, I hesitated, trembling at what it would mean.

I didn't know how to be anything else.

I remembered a story I'd read in Voyage of the Dawn Treader, *where annoying cousin Eustace turns into a dragon when he steals a hidden treasure. After a humiliating existence, and many*

attempts to turn himself back into a boy, he encoun-
ters Aslan, a lion who symbolizes Jesus.

Aslan asks Eustice if he wants to be well—if he
wants to be whole. But he warns him that it will
be an excruciating process in which Eustice's very
being will be stripped to the core. Aslan explains
that he must tear the dragon scales off, and that only
his sharp claws can penetrate the thick exterior. As
Aslan begins, Eustace describes what he feels, "The
very first tear he made was so deep that I thought it
had gone right into my heart. And when he began
pulling the skin off, it hurt worse than anything I've
ever felt. The only thing that made me able to bear
it was just the pleasure of feeling the stuff peel off ...
He peeled the beastly stuff right off ... And there I
was as smooth and soft as a peeled switch."

Like Eustice, I had to decide if I wanted to be well.

It was in Fiji, while terribly afraid and feeling
like my skin was being peeled from my bones, that
I set down my identity as a victim and took up my
new identity. That day, I wrote down four things that
I began meditating on day and night:

✦ *I am mentally well*
✦ *I am whole and enough*
✦ *I am the daughter of the Most High King*
✦ *There is a Heavenly Father who wants me*

About that same time, I read Hosea 2:14-20 for
the first time, and I clung to it because I felt like it
was my story too.

In the verses, God talks with Hosea about his
plan to win back Hosea's unfaithful wife. God says,

"*I am now going to allure her; I will lead her into the desert and speak tenderly to her. There I will give her back her vineyards, and will make the Valley of Trouble a door of hope. There she will sing as in the days of her youth. And when that happens, she will no longer call me master, she will call me husband.*"

Sometimes God ordains the desert. Not because he's angry but because he desperately loves us and wants to cut away the thorns, the distractions, the anger, the pain. And in that ordained desert, the only way out is when you learn to let go, remembering what joy feels like. Experiencing such an intimate exchange with the One who truly loves you allows you to look at God not as a disinterested master, but as a lover and a husband who longs to see you healthy and whole.

Figuratively, God drew me out to the desert, where I wandered for years and years, until I reached the end of myself. I was tired, exhausted by the situation with my father and my crippling anger; I was weak, and almost dead. Then he began to speak tenderly to me, and I listened. And he gave me back my joy. Out there, out where it was dry, I quit calling him master and I started calling him husband. I believe it's in the struggle and the fight that we finally learn how much he loves us—where we finally hear him say, "Draw near and listen. I have not abandoned you."

When I came home from Fiji, the circumstances in my family hadn't changed.

But I had.

Reality soon hit hard, and I felt myself re-entering that desert and forgetting my joy. But I fought and I dug deep and I yelled and I kicked and I worked on myself and I reflected and I sobbed and I prayed. Oh, how I prayed.

There's immense power in choice. And I now know that it was my choice—and mine alone—to live in freedom, to let go of anger, and to redefine my identity. It took years of discipline and hard work to remold my muscle memory of brokenness. But once I began to change, my family began to change, too.

In time, I received a gift I never expected. After decades of living in a drug-induced fog, my dad reached the end of himself and began his own journey toward healing. Under the close supervision of doctors and nurses, who helped him manage his pain with different medication, he emerged clearer-minded than he'd been in years. To us, this was everything. It signaled the end of what we refer to as "The Dark Ages" and the beginning of my family's own enlightenment. Dad's healing began, his personality returned, and his willingness to talk and own his own mistakes gradually unfolded.

My battle for wholeness cried out for authenticity and confession. I needed my family to have the conversations we couldn't have until dad decided he wanted to be well and was willing to re-engage with our family. Fueled by decades of unexpressed emotions, at last my family was able to have the raw, painful, vulnerable conversations that would allow us to walk down the long road of healing.

Through God's grace, my freedom created a ripple effect that eventually led to my family's freedom.

Families get well one member at a time.

Gretchen's grit and determination to learn what being well meant for her will continue to have ripple effects for generations. She is breaking the patterns that brought pain and dysfunction into her family with open communication, and she is a living example of why choosing to be well is so important for all of us—as well as those we love.

CHAPTER 11

What to Do with the Anger

*"Depression, suffering and anger are
all part of being human."*
Janet Fitch

I n every journey involving pain, there inevitably comes a time
when we have to figure out what to do with our anger. Like all
survivors, I could not control the circumstances that caused
my pain, but I *could* choose how to respond.

Years ago, before all the dark years, if anyone asked me if I
was angry, I would have denied it. I loved life. I loved having
fun. I was social and truly cannot recall ever feeling an emotion I could identify as anger. But anger can be a symptom
of internal pain turned outward, and, likewise, depression can
be the result of anger turned inward. Anger's expression can
come in many forms, depending on personalities and circum-

stances, but it is a normal reaction to any story of pain, fear, loss, abuse, or trauma.

After Jonas and I got married, if he did anything I didn't like I would "have a spunker," as he called it. I never said an unkind word during those times ... because I didn't say any words at all. If he came home late and dinner was cold, I would fall silent. That silence might last as long as two days. As I look back now, I realize that was anger. I didn't know how to verbalize what I was feeling, so instead, I would completely shut down. As far as I knew, that was normal.

I distinctly remember the first time I was aware of my anger. Angie was just a toddler and had been coughing terribly for several weeks. I kept thinking it was a bad cold and would eventually pass. Then two different friends of mine said something about how hard she was coughing and seemed concerned. I made a doctor's appointment and took Angie that same day. While I was sitting in the waiting room with her, the doctor heard her coughing and asked me to bring her back to a treatment room right away. After just a quick look, he informed me that Angie had whooping cough. He recognized her cough from practicing medicine overseas and immediately wrote a prescription for her.

That night I was furious with myself. I told Jonas how terrible I felt for letting her condition go on so long before asking for help. She could have died! We started the medicine right away and she started feeling better quickly.

The first time she slept through the night without coughing was the night before her tragic accident.

Already angry with myself on that terrible Monday morning, Angie's accident brought my feelings of inadequacy to the surface. My guilt reinforced the lie that I was not a good mom ...

that I could have prevented the accident ... If only I had called her back ... If only I walked the short distance to my parents' house with her instead of going inside to clean the kitchen ... Those thoughts would haunt me 24 hours a day for years, but still I buried them. I knew as far back as I could remember that "good girls don't get angry." So, I refused to identify any of the feelings I had as anger. I just remember feeling like I had a pit in my stomach. I now understand that anger was that pit.

Now that I can see that, I also see how I constantly tried to push my anger down. Still, it was always there, simmering just below the surface. For years, my anger leaked out through behaviors such as control, silence, sharp words, complaining, and whining. Living with unresolved anger was part of my daily life. It was my normal.

Five years after Angie's accident, when LaVale was very young, I remember trying to get her dressed for school, brushing her hair, but she was unhappy and kept resisting. As her frustration escalated, so did mine. In a weak moment, my deeper anger came bursting out, and I threw the brush down on the bathroom counter and it broke. And as I stood there, heart pounding, I was shocked that I had the capacity to hurt this little girl who I loved so much. Her lack of cooperation that day was a normal childhood behavior, yet it triggered an emotional volcano. That's when I began to understand that I didn't know how to manage my anger, all this emotion inside me.

Many years later, my counselor was the first person who told me that anger is a God-given emotion. In fact, our emotions are extremely helpful in bringing attention to the things that are getting in the way of our health—mentally, spiritually, emotionally, and even physically. He would tell me that "Anger makes a terrible master, but an excellent servant."

Letting anger run my life would be destructive but learning to use it appropriately would mean acknowledging and expressing those feelings in ways that actually help me create much-needed change in my life.

Denying or suppressing my anger only gave it a place to grow, and I learned the hard way how dangerous that can be. I learned that attuning my body and mind to my emotions is the only way to be fully alive. I had to be keenly aware of how my emotions are in play at all times. What I know about them and what I do with them are my responsibilities.

I'm grateful for the example about anger that Jesus gave us when he confronted the money changers in the temple. In the story, He saw them misusing the Temple for personal and financial gain, and he immediately protested. He turned over tables and rebuked the money changers openly for making His Temple into a den of thieves (I have to wonder if he turned over the tables not only because he was angry, but to expose the money being exchanged under the table).

In short, Jesus expressed His anger directly to those who were doing wrong. He did not delay, or stuff it down and whine. He did not use insults, threats, or gossip to let off steam. He allowed his anger to work for him that day. By doing so, He not only got the attention of the moneychangers, but he caused them to stop doing evil in His Father's house.

Knowing how Jesus felt seeing the temple used for selfish gain, I can't help but imagine what He would have done if he walked into our church in the early 1970's to find Pastor using his power and position to commit evil acts. As I began to speak the truth about my abuse—what it did to the church, to me, and to other women I cared about—my anger was redirected to the proper source. Anger served me well the day I was finally able to walk away from my abuser.

When I finally parted ways with my pastor, I asked him to meet me at a restaurant. As soon as we were both seated, I told him, "I'm not going to see you anymore."

He laughed at me. Then he said, "You'll never make it without me."

He took his wallet out of his pocket and showed me a stack of checks, indicating that he could provide for me financially if I would stay. But, by then, I knew it was nothing more than another tactic.

The day I walked away from him, I let anger work *for* me. For the first time in my life, I made the powerful choice to direct my anger at the source of my pain, rather than letting the emotional debris hurt everyone *but* him. I didn't feel the need to throw anything, scream at him, or pay him back for the pain he caused me. I simply told the truth and walked away.

I have never forgotten the power I felt in that moment. Anger served me well that day.

My sister, Fi, who helped me reach that important turning point to break free from Pastor, has battled anger since she was very young. Though we grew up in the same household, we have very different experiences regarding anger.

Anger was the only emotion I could feel for years after Angie's death. Although, emotions annoyed me, so I simply shut them all down ... well all except the anger. Every emotion I didn't want to feel somehow came out as anger.

But my battle with anger started long before adulthood.

I was a tomboy, always running and playing with my brothers. My father often took us ice skating in the winter, and there were so many fun memories. But for some reason I constantly battled feelings of intense rage. The smallest things would frustrate me. For example, our dad mowed the lawn in a sporadic pattern instead of straight rows and he never trimmed the edges, and that drove me crazy! In a family of five boys and three girls, chaos and messes were a daily reality, but I couldn't stand the messy house. Sometimes when I felt the anger building, I would go into my room and bite on a tennis ball as hard as I could. I was trying to release my frustration without anyone knowing.

I felt as if I was fighting an invisible enemy, long before the years of abuse by our pastor. Like a light switch that could flip at any moment, something as insignificant as a car pulling out in front of me in traffic could send me into a fit of rage without warning.

My husband, Mike, got the brunt of my outbursts for many years. Our marriage had so many factors working against it from the start—my pain and his, his past and mine. So, when we finally began to seek counseling for our marriage, I kept feeling as if there was a missing piece in the puzzle of my life. Our counselor tried to help me uncover any childhood trauma that might explain my rage, but I couldn't recall anything.

Then, in 1997, a few days after Christmas, my siblings and their families were all gathered at my parents' house. Every corner of the house was packed with people. Babies were crawling around, teenagers and adults were gathered in groups, while a basketball game was getting started outdoors, in spite of the cold weather. Over the laughter and conversations, the phone rang and soon I heard someone yell, "Fi! Telephone!"

I made my way through the crowded rooms toward the phone. I held the receiver up to one ear while covering the other, straining to hear over the chatter and laughter in the house. On the other end was someone I hadn't seen in years. He was 10 years older than I, but our families spent time together when I was very young. After a moment of small talk, the tone of his voice changed. He became very serious and started to explain the reason for his call.

I couldn't possibly have predicted what he would say next.

He said, "When you were three or four years old, a few of the other boys and I sexually abused you. I had to call and tell you ... I just had to tell you how sorry I am that this happened."

All the talking and noise in the room faded into the background as I tried to take in what he was saying. This was my missing puzzle piece.

He told me he would be happy to talk with me further if I needed to ask any questions, and I did eventually ask him what I was doing while the boys were attacking me. He told me, "You were mad! Kicking and screaming and yelling."

When Mike and I returned home after Christmas, I contacted our counselor and began trying to make sense of this new information. Somehow, dealing with the anger became easier when I realized that my brain had stored that memory, even though I was too young to remember or understand. I'd spent my life up to that point trying to control everything in an effort to protect myself against an unknown threat. Whenever I felt out of control or got backed into a corner, my brain automatically reacted in the same way it responded when I was fighting for my life as a child.

Even now, with that information, normal daily life occasionally triggers my anger. But now, when I feel anger suddenly rush to the surface, I can recognize it and release it. Understanding the reason for my angry reaction allows me to let it pass.

When children are violated before they can even comprehend trauma, the effects linger for the rest of their lives. And little girls are not the only survivors. It happens to one out of six boys, too[4].

My story, and many others included in this book, are from a female perspective. But so many of the men in our lives are dealing with the aftereffects of pain and trauma. Our brothers, fathers, sons, uncles, grandfathers, and friends are also struggling with what to do with the things they have experienced, and, so often, anger is what finally signals their need for help.

Todd is a social worker who realized his anger was becoming unmanageable only after years of trying to keep it at bay. Throughout his career, he helped countless people find resources during major life events, yet he continually tried to deal with his own internal crisis alone.

During a meeting at work, he was unjustifiably called out for something he couldn't control and completely lost his temper. In a room full of medical professionals and fellow social workers, he found himself yelling. That outburst scared him. It made him wonder what else he might be capable of doing, and that's when he decided to seek professional help. Todd shared with a counselor the painful memory of a 14-year-old neighbor molesting him in his own home when he was just six years old. That same neighbor came over on another day with his seven-year-old sister, forcing Todd to violate her while he watched.

Processing the abuse with an experienced therapist helped Todd understand how that trauma contributed to the depression he battled for years, as well as the anger that eventually resulted in his public outburst. The power of confession helped him grieve and allowed him to process his feelings of guilt. The shame of being part of something so ugly was deep. Todd was afraid that if he told his parents, they would think he was seeking attention, or conclude that he was weak, or might tell him he should have simply said "no."

When he was finally able to share his story with a few trusted people, no one thought he was weak or suggested that he should have done something differently. In fact, he says each time he shares his story, he feels a little bit freer and his voice gets a little bit stronger.

———•◆•———

Anger isn't always the result of abuse, and it isn't always as obvious as you might expect.

Emily is a friend of mine who grew up in a pastor's home like Todd, but she was not abused. She never identified herself as an angry person and, in fact, whenever conflict happened in her family, Emily was the one who stepped into the role of peacemaker. She kept a cool head and brought unity and understanding into whatever conflicts she faced. But inside, she was constantly frustrated and angry. She never had a public outburst, but when she was diagnosed with depression and an eating disorder in her mid-20's, she was surprised to discover how much anger she was internalizing, camouflaged underneath her calm demeanor.

The lack of control Emily felt over her life and the steady diet of criticism she and her family received in ministry, combined with beliefs that made her fearful of making mistakes, got to her. At first, perfectionism became her vice as an attempt to avoid criticism. She believed, "If I do things perfectly, no one will criticize me."

Perfection proved to be an illusion that left her constantly exhausted and discouraged. Since she couldn't be perfect, there were times when she wanted to be invisible instead. She became smaller and smaller physically as she tried to cope with the emotions she wouldn't allow herself to express outwardly. When she chose to begin healing, in addition to a support group and ongoing therapy, journaling became a safe outlet for her. She began writing with depth and honesty as part of her healing and learned to use her gift for words to identify and express her emotions in ways that not only helped her, but eventually helped others as well. Today, she is a professional writer who helps others tell their stories. In fact, she is the co-writer of *The Secret Lies Within*. She also speaks and sings, even when fear tries to keep her quiet.

The truth is, none of us can "control" our anger if we want to experience genuine peace. We must acknowledge our anger, identify the sources of pain that drive it, and use it wisely to help our situation. It is not meant to be a constant companion, but more of an ambulance that drives us to a place of safety and health. Anger provides an energy meant to spur us toward a more productive resolution.

The internal war we wage against all the unfairness, the shame, the way we wish things could be, will never be won by staying angry. But when we decide to feel it, mourn whatever brought it on, and express it in a helpful way, we finally start to release it back into the wild.

CHAPTER 12

Making Peace with the Pain

*"Even the saddest things can become,
once we have made peace with them,
a source of wisdom and strength for the
journey that still lies ahead."*
Frederick Buechner

When we experience hurt of any kind, it is so easy to jump to the conclusion that God wasn't really there. I had the same questions anyone asks in the middle of pain:

Was He punishing me?
Didn't I pray hard enough?
Was there something wrong with me?
Why couldn't I feel him near me
when I cried out to him?

**Wasn't there another way for me to learn what
I learned as a result of that pain?**

The questions get especially complicated when people claiming to speak for God inflict pain on us:

Is God abusive?
Does He hate me?
**How can I believe He is loving when He
lets terrible things like this happen?**
Is He even there at all?
Who can I trust?

Knowing Jesus had questions for His Father—questions very much like mine—helps me trust Him with my questions. The night Jesus was arrested, He agonized over all that was happening and asked His Father if there was any other way.

In the intensely painful moments just before Jesus died, He felt His Father's eyes turn away from His suffering and He begged, "My God, My God, why have you forsaken me?" (Matthew 27:46)

I have asked that same question. But this scene in Jesus's story reveals a deeply personal observation to me: that His Father understands, like no one else, the strange dissonance of sorrow mingled with love that made me want to look away from my own child's lifeless body.

He gets it.

I can't explain all the mysteries of God. I'm no theologian. But I know what I have experienced. In the midst of the worst mess imaginable is where I found Him. And He was more loving and trustworthy than I ever knew. It was only in my pain that I found my connection with Him, and, eventually, my connection with others. For too long, I could only see the world through the dark lens of my pain. Slowly, each truth, each confession, each forgiveness, each step toward wholeness allowed a little more light into my life.

Back when I was begging God to remove my grief and clean up the mess shame made of my life, I never imagined that I would eventually make peace with all that pain. Over time, I stopped focusing on removing the pain and began asking what it could teach me. And I discovered something far more miraculous than God removing all my pain ... I realized that He could redeem it.

———•◦•———

Redemption in no way suggests perfection. We don't learn anything from perfection.

Rather, redemption is what happens when the script changes and we can finally experience the beauty that is possible *because of* the pain, rather than *in spite of* it. I couldn't have predicted how the pain that isolated me would later facilitate a deep sense of connectedness with God and other people. The secrets that once kept me stuck in isolation now compel me to strive for a life of authenticity. The very story I was tempted to escape altogether actually shaped me into someone who can make a difference in the world.

My sisters and I have incrementally made peace with our pain in different ways and on different timelines. We have all come through the pain of our stories with different perspectives and reactions to the things we experienced. More than 35 years after Becky walked away from Pastor, she experienced a breakthrough moment where she finally saw how her pain was redeemed in a way she never expected.

> *When my kids were teenagers (17 and 19) my hus-band, Aaron, and I shared our story with them at the dinner table one evening. Aaron told them, "You can ask us any questions you want to ask, and we will be honest with you, but I will not allow you to hold this over your mother's head for the rest of her life."*
>
> *The kids honored his request and I am grateful for the respect that both my son and daughter have shown me. We did not have many conversations about it after that night, until December 2017.*
>
> *Aaron and I were visiting our son and his wife over the Christmas holiday when a conversation opened up very naturally about those rocky years. It was sweet and hard. There were tears. They were both very kind and asked thoughtful questions. If they asked me anything I couldn't talk about, they were understanding. I took that opportunity to tell my son how sorry I was for not being there for him during those years when he was young. I was gone all the time. All of us who were caught in the trap of the pastor's control were constantly preoccupied and unavailable to our families.*
>
> *And he unexpectedly said: "That's okay, Mom. You're here for me now."*
>
> *He went on to tell me how much it meant to him that his parents are still together after all these years, especially after the obstacles we faced. He and his wife shared that among their group of*

friends, which includes six or seven couples, all of their friends' parents are divorced except his. He expressed so beautifully how he would rather have me here for him now and for me and Aaron to still be together.

Anne often tells her story publicly to large audiences, and she and Fi have both written and published their stories. I have only shared parts of my story at certain times to certain people when I knew my experiences could help them.

Anne believes firmly in the power of confession and what it has meant in her life, and now I understand more fully. The truth really did set me free. I've heard about grace all my life, but that day with my son and his wife, I experienced it more powerfully than ever. A few years before that conversation, I had a conversation with my daughter and shared some similar things with her. The conversation with my son and his wife allowed me to move into a whole new place of healing that has provided so much relief.

I thought I would be done with all this by now. But when I look back, I know I am a better person because of what happened to me.

I can tell you that no one heals overnight. It is a process. For so long, I had a hard time accepting grace. I remember feeling like I was rotten to the core and didn't deserve grace. Eventually, I came to realize that no one else could fix this for me or give me permission to accept the grace I'd been given. I had to walk through this myself with God.

> *I remember saying to God, "Either you're the God you say you are, or you're not."*
>
> *Now, finally, I can tell you that He is. And if He can redeem my story, He can redeem anything.*

I will always remember the call I got from Becky telling me about that experience. I was overjoyed for her. And I do agree— He really can redeem anything.

Fi and her husband, Mike, have each experienced a story of pain most of us could never fathom, and making peace with their pain has been an uphill journey. After decades of feeling nothing but anger, Fi writes:

> *I feel other emotions now, including gratitude. I'm grateful for healing. I'm grateful that, in spite of all the pain and anger, I was spared the added horror of addiction. It's ironic, really, that the same upbringing that kept me from talking about my pain also helped shield me from substance abuse, which I could have easily fallen into if I had access to drugs or alcohol.*
>
> *I'm grateful for the phone call back in 1997 that helped me make sense of all the rage. And I'm incredibly grateful for a husband who stayed with me through it all, forgave me for everything I did that caused him pain, and still loves me today. I'm grateful for the support of our family and for the God who met me in my pain and led me to safety.*

Owning our own story also helps us recognize pain in others and being in tune and brave enough to reach out to someone might even save a life. I think of the phone call I received from Chub during the depths of my despair and I hope I can be as in tune to others who need to hear the voice of hope as he was the day he called me. I think of the day, many years after Angie died, when Jonas became a first responder after a tragic Amish schoolhouse shooting. He stood with parents who lost their daughter and offered empathy and comfort. It is in those moments that I realize our pain was not a waste, but it prepared us for specific purposes.

LaWonna and LaVale have experienced more heartache than anyone should have to in one lifetime. I have cried rivers of tears over the pain they experienced. As much as I wish I could remove all their hurts, I can't. They are now incredible women who have experienced losses and trauma and I stand in awe of their resilience.

Jonas and I always hoped our daughters would see the beauty and value inside themselves. Now they have kids of their own. One day, LaWonna sent us an email that made us incredibly happy. She told us she had been handing out tiaras to her daughters and their friends and shared the story behind it.

Without a doubt, the most difficult challenge I have faced was when we were trying to decide if we should leave Pennsylvania. This meant leaving all of my family and close friends and moving to a place where we knew not one single person ... a much-needed fresh start. After much prayer, debate, and thought, my husband and I decided it would be the best thing for us. We were doing it. We had to for the sake of our children and each other. It was simply time to go.

Due to circumstances beyond our control, the decision to stay or go had to be made in about four days. Our house sold about 20 days later, then we had an additional 30 days to pack and be out of our home. It was a whirlwind.

The process of packing and moving a very large home with numerous out buildings, leaving the family business, leaving family, leaving the home that we poured blood, sweat, and tears into, was overwhelming (not to mention my children and their friends and what they were going through). My husband was not physically well and, while he did what he could, the bulk of the task rested on my shoulders. There were times when this daunting process became unbearable. I'm not very good at doing the emotional part of things and, for whatever reason, this was incredibly emotional for me.

It still is.

The move wore me down physically, mentally, emotionally, and spiritually. Anything and everything that could have gone wrong did! We got a record snowfall, my kids were out of school five weeks before we left because they were dog sick, dates were changing, and vehicle issues came up ... blah, blah, blah. It was hard on all of us.

One particular day I woke up feeling extremely overwhelmed and burdened and I just didn't want to do it that day. As I got out of the shower and was getting dressed I was really struggling with feeling completely furious, and I was clearly furious at God. I felt like I had endured enough in one lifetime *to last me the entire rest of mine, plus some. I just wanted somebody to give me a break. It was a total pity party for one.*

As I was getting dressed, I heard an unmistakable Voice say, "Put on your armor."

Of course, I battled with this, pretending not to hear. To my dismay, it just got louder and clearer. So I said, "Fine. I'll put on my armor."

In my head, I went through the process I learned long ago from Ephesians 6: the shield, the helmet, the sword, the breast plate, etc. When I was finished with all that, I hear, "Where is your crown?"

Again, I tried to ignore the Voice, but it was just so loud and clear that I again succumbed and went and got a tiara that I had sitting up on a shelf collecting dust.

I said, "Fine, I will wear it for a little while ... just for You. But only a little while."

And so, I did.

The next morning when I woke up, I did it again ... and the day after that, and the day after that.

What I found happening really caught me off guard. So, I asked Him, "Lord, why on earth must I wear this tiara?"

"Are you not the daughter of the most high King?"

"Yes, Lord I am."

"Does not that not make you royalty? Does that not make you my princess?"

To which I replied, "Yes, Lord, it does. Thank you. I get it now."

I began to wear that ridiculous tiara two or three times a week. Sometimes more, sometimes less. I began to feel stronger, protected, calmer, more productive, and really quite royal! If I had not begun to feel that way, I have no doubt I would have crumbled, just completely lost it.

As all this was transpiring, I stumbled onto a book by Marianne Williamson, who wrote A Woman's Worth *and* A Return to Love, *and I was so inspired by her words. Her perspective confirmed everything I was feeling. She talks about the difference between a princess and a queen and asks why the word "princess" is so often used to describe a certain type of woman, but rarely the word "queen." The book talked about the princess as a girl who knows she will get there but isn't there yet—who doesn't yet know how to use her power responsibly or express her pain constructively.*

"To be a princess is to play at life," she writes. "To be a queen is to be a serious player ... A queen is wise. She has earned her serenity, not having had it bestowed on her but having passed her tests. She has suffered and grown more beautiful because of it ... She cares deeply about something bigger than herself. She rules with authentic power."

After reading that, I promptly started making my girls wear tiaras too! (I cannot stress enough how important it was to explain to them that we are NOT talking fairytale princesses here!). Now, whenever appropriate, I give tiaras to their friends and explain why. How will they know how amaz-

ing they are—and will continue to be—if we do not teach them?

(If you have boys, don't worry, there are crowns for them too!)

I honestly believe this is my mission in life: to outfit every woman and girl with a tiara. I profoundly believe it could change who we are as a society.

Wearing this tiara has changed my entire perspective about how special I am in His eyes. When I am weary as a mother, weary with life, laundry, dishes, the never-ending responsibilities, the demands we face every day, I honest to God put this silly tiara on. I have even been known to go out and about, I'm talking grocery shopping, with this thing on my head! I have, in fact, worn it all day on more than one occasion, talking to neighbors, people I work with, going to the bank, running errands, etc.

I have even become annoyed at people for their looks and stares, wondering, "What the heck are they looking at?"

My husband has come home to me vacuuming in a tiara, all the while I was completely oblivious that it was still on my head. It feels like it should be there. It feels like I am, in fact, a queen in my home and my daughters are princesses. It has brought out my feminine side. I am more confident, more tolerant, more loving, and I'd like to think more patient (although I'm not sure my kids would agree).

There are still many, many days when I simply need to be reminded that I AM the daughter of the most high King. I AM special, and oh so valued by

Him. I AM his child and that truly does make me a princess.

You MUST have a tiara. It is my hope that it will do the same for you. I leave you with one last quote from Marianne Williamson:

"Our deepest fear is not that we are inadequate. Our deepest fear is that we are powerful beyond measure. It is our light, not our darkness that most frightens us. We ask ourselves, 'Who am I to be brilliant, gorgeous, talented, fabulous?' Actually, who are you not to be? You are a child of God. Your playing small does not serve the world. There is nothing enlightened about shrinking so that other people won't feel insecure around you. We are all meant to shine, as children do. We were born to make manifest the glory of God that is within us. It's not just in some of us; it's in everyone. And as we let our own light shine, we unconsciously give other people permission to do the same. As we are liberated from our own fear, our presence automatically liberates others."

Those tiaras are helping LaWonna remember what is true— not only about herself but her children and the other lives she impacts. She is allowing her life's experiences help her live a better story.

That is redemption.

There was one day when Jonas was reminiscing while mowing the lawn, and this thought came to him: "The rich things

I learned from the worst day of my life make me thankful for the memory of them."

It took a long time for that statement to become true for us. But now, in this stage of our lives, we can say it and *mean* it.

It is impossible to make sense of all the tragedy in this world, yet it *is* possible to come to some level of peace. When we let pain define us, we get stuck. When we try to solve or prevent it, we get disappointed. But when we begin to make peace with our pain, transformation becomes possible at last.

CHAPTER 13

Embracing Freedom

*"Free yourself, like a gazelle from
the hand of the hunter,
like a bird from the snare of the fowler."*
Proverbs 6:5

A longing for freedom is hardwired into our DNA. From the moment we leave our mother's womb and come screaming into this world, we are designed to grow into people who are free to live stories that have meaning and purpose in the grand scheme of things.

If you've ever seen a toddler break free from his or her parents and go careening out of control, you've seen how the freedom for which we are *designed* is not always a freedom for which we are *ready*. That same ache for freedom explains countless stories of teenagers who sneak out into the dark of night, trying to taste freedom but only getting its counterfeit (and probably even fewer privileges as a result of their disobedience). It is important to acknowledge that our *longing* for freedom is not what gets us into trouble. We run into trouble when we try to pursue freedom without the wisdom and boundaries that help us fulfill a grander purpose. Freedom isn't about escaping our life but fully engaging with it.

Confession, for me, was like walking over a shaky, rope bridge suspended over the Grand Canyon, and on the other side of that bridge was a whole new world that began my journey of recovery.

Once the truth was out, and I was open to the possibility of being forgiven, I began to see the world from a completely different vantage point. I was no longer constantly trying to manage lies or escape reality, so I was able to be more present in the here and now. I began to experience the freedom I always hoped for but couldn't while in the dark.

I discovered that, rather than trying to free myself *from* my life, I was free *for* my life, a more satisfying life, brimming with purpose. I no longer wanted to live vicariously through soap operas or find other means of escape to fantasize about the life I wanted.

I no longer had to arrange for babysitters in order to pacify a predator.

The late Brennan Manning was a recovering alcoholic whose colorful redemption story is told through the numerous books he wrote before he passed away. He states so beautifully the internal shift that leads to true freedom:

> "A gradual transformation takes place in the process of confession. We go from an attitude of self-hatred to an attitude of self-acceptance. Self-acceptance is not being self-centered. When we accept ourselves for who we are we cease to hunger for power or

acceptance of others. We no longer care about being popular or powerful. We are not afraid of criticism and we no longer desire to please others. Being true to ourselves brings inner and lasting peace. Accepting ourselves allows us to choose acceptable behavioral patterns that are beneficial to ourselves and others."[5]

Embracing freedom meant setting boundaries for myself. Boundaries are like guardrails we put into place that help us make choices that lead us in the direction we want to go. Freedom *from* boundaries, I learned, only led to disaster. I needed those boundaries, so I could walk forward into the life I fought so hard to save. Those boundaries helped me rebuild trust with Jonas and with my family, and they helped me develop new habits that would keep me from sabotaging my own life.

———◆———

Breaking my silence and taking responsibility for my choices helped me find my voice.

And finding my voice gave me opportunities to tell my story.

I found that the more I shared my story, the more people I met who needed to tell theirs. I started groups where women could share their stories in a safe setting, and I was amazed to see how their lives began to change as a result of sharing their stories. My friend, Kate, is one of those women. We grew up in the same community and shared similar backgrounds, but I had no idea how my story would free her to live out her own dreams. Kate joined the very first group I formed and was able to safely share her story.

Growing up as a little Amish girl, I felt sheltered and protected from the world. Family is very important to the Amish and we were always surrounded by not only our immediate family but grandparents and cousins as well. We took care of each other and enjoyed being together. We very seldom heard our parents telling us they loved us—talking about feelings and emotions just didn't happen often—but we knew we were loved and wanted. I never doubted that for a moment.

I grew up in a good home with no abuse of any kind. I don't remember my parents ever raising their voices at each other or at us. We were provided for and never felt in need of anything.

But in the midst of that safe environment, my parents couldn't protect us from everything. The first time I ever felt unsafe was when I was in second grade and my younger brother and I rode the school bus. Some of the children made it their obligation to torture us Amish kids on the bus and seemed to delight in the fact that they could do anything they wanted, knowing we wouldn't fight back.

The Amish are a peace-loving people, and the parents of these bullies would have made our parents' lives miserable. That had happened quite often in the past. So, we suffered in silence until our parents placed us in another school. Looking back now, I realize that even though my parents' hands were tied, I started feeling unprotected unless I stood up for myself.

A few years later, I was back to feeling struck again—bullying at its finest, although back then *we didn't call it that. In junior high, I became the daily target of a boy who must've felt the need to be mean to someone and I was his victim for an extended period of time. He called me names and did whatever he thought would make me miserable. He even resorted to accusing me of stealing money off his desk. He was a popular "class clown" and the teacher believed him without ever listening to my side of the story.*

When my parents were told, they believed me. But they never stood up for me to the teacher.

Once again, I felt very unprotected and unheard.

I was part of the generation that didn't talk to their parents about feelings and I definitely didn't try to after that. I realize now that I built a wall to protect myself lest anyone else hurt me. I also realized that, because I was a girl, I was supposed to be the "weaker" sex. It wasn't accepted in our culture for a girl to be outspoken, or even to have opinions.

But I was not your "normal" conservative girl at heart. I had dreams and wanted to go places. I wanted to go to high school and graduate but didn't have a say in the matter and had to quit school after the 8th grade. I had a restlessness inside, which I didn't understand at that time. I did what all Amish girls do: got a job, got married young, and started a family.

Although I loved being a mom and wife, and wouldn't change that for anything, I still longed for more. I felt a sense of calling to ministry. I wanted to journey alongside other women and had a deep compassion for women who were hurting and wounded. I felt especially drawn to those within the traditional conservative realm, whose dreams and spirits have been crushed by conservative leaders. In my case, those leaders were all men in the church who were quick to say that women could not be in any kind of ministry or leadership position in the church. We were to be submissive to our husbands and to the leaders, regardless of what we felt called to do. We were made to feel inferior within the church setting, so I kept building up walls around my heart until, eventually, my calling to help other women had all but died. I no longer felt it.

Through all of this, my dear husband supported and encouraged my vision. We came to realize that we needed to leave that restricted, traditional church setting. In time, we started going to the same church as Anne. I had always known her since we basically grew up together, but we'd lost track of one another over the years. I have no doubt God caused our paths to cross at just this time in my life because He knew I would need her help to survive what was about to happen.

Not long after we started attending that church, my husband and I were out on our motorcycles, enjoying a nice summer evening, when I crashed. I suffered many injuries, including a severe head injury, and ended up severely depressed. Now I realize that depression was not only the result of my head trauma but was also the result of me no longer being able to suppress the resentment for the oppression *that built up over the years. I was no longer able to maintain that wall of protection around my heart.*

Around that time, I started attending a class where a small group of women could share our stories in a safe environment, and I shared my story for the very first time. It was one of the hardest things I have ever done. I did not like to talk about myself or draw any attention to myself (and I still don't), but I felt safe there.

That was the first time I ever felt safe enough to talk about my feelings to anyone other than my husband. The women in that group believed in me and saw something in me I no longer saw in myself. That vision that was still deep down in my soul was rekindled. They encouraged me, challenged me, and helped me pick up the shattered pieces of my self-esteem. They loved me unconditionally, gave me pep talks, affirmed my vision, and helped me realize that women CAN have callings from God and pursue them. At last, I could see the value in myself that no one could suppress or take away.

I learned that God calls both men and women to do His work. In His eyes, we are all created equal and can work together to build his kingdom. One is not better or above the other, but we complement each other.

In time, this little Amish girl with the desire to journey with hurting women grew to embrace that calling.

I still do not like the word "submission," and at times I still feel that veil of oppression creeping over my spirit in certain settings. I will always have to fight depression, but because I believe in myself and have no doubt that my Creator desires for me to live in freedom, I will fight until my last breath and continue to choose joy as long as I am on this earth.

I still hate bullying and do everything in my power to stand up for the victims, who have included my own grandchildren at times. Because I know how bullying feels, I refuse to stand by silently! I am learning to speak up for myself and others. I now know that can be done in a kind, constructive way and that God wants me to do that. There are still so many hurting women out there who need to find peace and freedom, and I still have a heart for those conservative women who desire to find their voice.

In my groups, I often tell women like Kate:

**"Life is hard, but God is good.
Don't confuse the two."**

I'm always surprised by the number of people I meet who think they don't have a story. The truth is, every one of us is living out a unique story. Whether the details of our stories are similar or different, your story is your own and it is an important part of a much larger story. None of us live in a vacuum. Our stories overlap and affect each other in more ways than we can ever fully comprehend.

Our stories are not meant to be compared; they are meant to be shared.

It is never about simply telling the facts and timelines of our lives; it's also about the vulnerability that comes with sharing the things that weigh us down and get us stuck.

Freedom calls to us through each other's stories. As we are able to tell the truth, vulnerability softens us and readies us for healing. And healing begins to offer us freedom—freedom that lets us decide how our stories will end.

CHAPTER 14

Rewriting Your Ending

"When we deny the story, it defines us.
When we own the story, we can write
a brave new ending."
Brené Brown

As Jonas and I found healing for ourselves and for our marriage, a dream took root in Jonas's heart to become a counselor and provide counseling services to the Amish community.

To make ends meet while he was studying, I started working for a farmer's market stand in Maryland. As a young Amish girl, I spent a great deal of time working in farmer's markets, so I was comfortable in that setting and worked hard to help my employer succeed. Rather than baking pies and cakes as I did as a child, this time I learned the art of making hand-rolled, soft pretzels.

After only one day, the owner was so pleased with my work that he asked me to be the manager. The more responsibility I gained, the more my confidence grew. The stand became more and more successful and I started managing other employees who came along to help the growing business.

After I had been managing that stand for a while, a young girl whom I'd met at the farmer's market told me that a family who owned a similar stand had just put their business on the market. She told me I should consider buying it.

I shrugged it off at first. I'd never even considered owning a business before, but this new opportunity would be closer to home. The more I thought about it, the more curious I became. I called the owners and learned that their price for the market stand was $6,000, and by the end of that short phone conversation, Jonas and I decided to buy it.

We bought the store sight unseen.

Still, $6,000 seemed like an insurmountable obstacle. We were living paycheck to paycheck and $6,000 might as well have been a million dollars for us at the time.

We knew there was no bank that would offer us a loan, so we had to find another option. At the time, Jonas's parents were the only people we knew would have the money and we felt strongly they would loan it to us. But we had never asked anyone for money. It went against our very nature, but we knew this is what we wanted to do. With my heart pounding and sweaty palms, I was able to muster the courage to ask his father.

Immediately he said, "I believe I can loan it to you."

So, within 24 hours of buying the stand, we were sitting with his parents at their kitchen table, his father handing me a check for $6,000.

I told him, "Pop, I don't know when we will be able to pay you back. We don't have anything."

He told me that he trusted us, and he knew we would pay him back whenever we could.

The check felt heavy in my hands. I had never held that much money in my life. And, just like that, we were buying our own business!

Our new market stand was located in Downingtown, Pennsylvania, a small town just off Route 30. The previous owners had offered pizza, pretzels, ice cream, and drinks. It was one of the larger locations in the market and, compared to the stand I had been working for, this market was older, a bit tired and run-down. Jonas and I tried to keep an optimistic attitude about this new adventure, but the atmosphere certainly put a damper on our enthusiasm at first. But we set in to clean, renovate, and refresh the stand and Jonas found ways to make operations run smoothly.

That first day in my stand, I was so nervous and hoped we had made the right decision. Early that first morning, a bouquet of roses was delivered with a note:

You can do this, honey.
Love, Jonas

It was a relief when customers showed up that first day, but after a few weeks, I could see all the potential at this stand. The stand got busier each week and family members began to jump in and help us. Fi became the pizza chef and LaVale and LaWonna helped me run the stand, along with a couple of my nieces.

But there was a problem. While the pizza was great, the pretzels tasted horrible.

We sold more and more pizzas each week and I decided to take the pretzels off the menu when Jonas got a little sparkle in his eye and asked if he could try changing up the recipe before we decided not to sell any more pretzels. I told him that if he thought it was a great idea, go for it (I secretly didn't know how he could possibly save the pretzels).

But, there he was, quietly starting to concoct a new pretzel recipe. And when we pulled the first tray out of the oven, they looked and smelled delicious. We couldn't wait to taste them. And once we did, we couldn't stop eating them! Jonas and I knew we were onto something. He suggested that we not tell anyone what we had done with the recipe.

And he was right. We didn't have to advertise. The smell of the pretzels immediately drew customers and word quickly spread.

There is just no way to describe an Auntie Anne's pretzel unless you have tasted it for yourself.

Yes. It's true. That little stand I bought in 1988, combined with the irresistible pretzel recipe Jonas concocted, grew into the international franchise known as Auntie Anne's Hand-rolled Soft Pretzels. Eventually, we would have Auntie Anne's stores in 48 states and 25 countries.

How does a woman with an eighth-grade education, who knows nothing about business, ever prepare for this kind of twist in her story? I couldn't have possibly dreamed big enough to imagine how the little girl who once baked pies for the market in her family's basement kitchen would grow to become the owner of Auntie Anne's Pretzels.

Really, I know that Auntie Anne's was about far more than pretzels, money, or success. The franchise was born out of a story of redemption that needed to be shared. Only through the unexpected success of Auntie Anne's could I speak in front of large audiences and share my story on national television.

God gave me a pretzel,
then He gave me a platform.

Those early days were hectic and intense as we tried to keep up with the rapid growth. During that time, Jonas was completing his counseling courses while also building the first 25-30 Auntie Anne storefronts. He did all that while also working with couples in counseling. Eventually, the success of Auntie Anne's allowed Jonas to fulfill his dream of building a community counseling center that met the needs of our community, including those in the Amish culture who didn't trust outside counselors.

Jonas often says, "I knew I had successfully done what I set out to do when I pulled up to the community center one morning and saw a buggy in the parking lot."

While the success came with wonderful opportunities, it also came with a price of its own. Money and success do not solve the problems inside us. In fact, business can serve to camouflage our problems. The explosive growth of Auntie Anne's became difficult to manage during the years depression and pain were part of my daily life. For 17 years, we continued to build Auntie Anne's Hand-Rolled Soft Pretzels. Then in 2005, we made the difficult decision to sell the company. We felt like we had taken it as far as we wanted to take it and knew it was time to move on.

When we walked away, after all those years, we left well. We built something wonderful, and now we can honestly say that even more wonderful than the success of Auntie Anne's is the life Jonas and I have built together. We have come to a place in our lives where we are finally beginning to grasp that our inner life is far more important than our outer world.

It was the difficult inner work that helped me rewrite the rest of my story, not anything that was happening outwardly. My greatest success is not Auntie Anne's, the company.

It is Auntie Anne, the person.

CHAPTER 15

It's Just Not Perfect Here

"Out of suffering have emerged the strongest souls;
the most massive characters are seared with scars."
Khalil Gibran

I want to be able to give you a happy ending to my story.
I have worked very hard to be able to write my own
ending and finish my journey well, but the reality of my
story is that I am still not sure how it all ends. There are many
days my heart still hurts.

But during one of the lowest moments in my life, Jonas said
something profound that gave me great comfort. He said:

> **"Hon, I'm so sorry this happened. I can't fix**
> **this for you. It's just not perfect here."**

He's right.

We live in a broken world, where so many things cannot be fixed. Often my expectations of this life are not realistic. I had to learn there are no quick solutions, nor are my prayers a vending machine for getting what I want. I can't undo what has been done to me, nor can I take away pain I have caused others. I can't get Angie back on this side of eternity.

None of us can prevent the tragedies, deaths, or pain that alter the course of our lives. Tragedy can happen to anyone at any time.

My friend, Katrina, vividly remembers the day a 7.0 earthquake in Haiti shook her life to its very foundation. She understands with painful clarity how this world can bring unspeakable pain and, in just a few seconds, forever change our lives.

I moved to Haiti when I was three years old. I never remembered having any other home than the one in Carrefour, Port-Au-Prince. My life was filled with change, adventure, cultures, miracles, testing the elements, physical strength, loving the poorest, and so much laughter. I wouldn't change anything about growing up in Haiti. I am eternally grateful to my parents for raising me the way they did. I have been given a broad view of the world and its people growing up in a missionary family.

When I was going to nursing school in Pennsylvania in January of 2010, a catastrophic earthquake hit Haiti. The day of the earthquake was my niece's tenth birthday. Our family didn't want to take away from her celebration as we learned what was happening. But with the news playing on a television in the living room, the reality started to sink in.

We got a phone call from Haiti telling us what happened and who was still alive. We learned that my brother and his wife, five of my closest friends, and our three-story home were all stripped away in a split second, and I felt the most heart-wrenching sorrow I have ever felt ... a bottomless sadness, too deep for words.

I haven't felt quite the same since the 14 seconds that shook the foundations of my world.

About five days after the earthquake, I went back to Haiti to help, thanks to a family friend who is a pilot. We stopped at an airport in the Bahamas while my friend worked to get us clearance to proceed into Haiti. It was dark by the time we finally hit the small, familiar runway. There were no customs, no paperwork, nothing official. A green Chevy truck pulled up and we loaded a few supplies into the back. After a nod from a Marine guard at the gate, we were out on the deserted, dusk-smitten streets of Port-Au-Prince.

On the drive to Carrefour, I rode between my two brothers, crying into their shoulders as the vehicle swerved here and there to avoid potholes and trash piles. It had been a long, hard week getting there but at last we piled out of the car in the beloved land of our youth. The smell of death was everywhere, the property where my cherished home once stood was a mountain of rubble and the dead bodies of people I loved.

I sank to the ground, sobs wracking my body, while my brother held me.

We didn't feel like sleeping, so we set out to the dirt streets of our neighborhood with flashlights. There was a lady with a child whose toe was crushed and filled with dirt and debris. The child screamed while her mother held her tight, so we could clean her wounds and bandage her toe. It seemed unfathomable that, almost a week after the quake, not even basic first aid had been provided.

The light of day revealed even more horror. It's difficult to describe the devastation. Dead bodies were everywhere, half-covered by rubble. Some people were barely alive when we found them, and supplies were sparse. Medical clinics were set up in tents and we did whatever we could to help as many as we could. I spent my days on the streets, scraping debris from people's wounds, cleaning them, bandaging them, often crying with them. We put together food packets for as many as possible and delivered them in secret to avoid riots.

Everywhere I turned, someone had lost even more than I had.

I was up most days at the crack of dawn, sometimes as early as 4:00 AM, and would work until midnight. Sometimes I look back and wonder how I kept going like that for so long. But the needs were great—greater than we could possibly meet. There was always someone to heal, help, feed, take to the hospital, translate for, or care for. All I could see was the person in front of me, every second, every hour. I put my own grief aside and kept going and going. Even now, the smells of the cleaning *supplies we used during the rescue and recovery efforts makes me gag, reminding me of the inescapable smell of death.*

Nothing could soothe my pain, so I tried escaping it. My life veered in ways I never thought I would take as I sank deeper and deeper into what felt like a dark, empty hole. Alcohol and parties with loud music couldn't drown out the pain, but I felt relieved when I could let go and forget the pain for even a few hours. Falling in love couldn't put anything back that was lost but having the love of a man in the midst of all the devastation gave me a reason to wake up.

So, I chose that life over the faith I'd always been taught to cling to in troubling times. After seeing so much human suffering, I felt like God was far away. I questioned everything I'd ever known. I wanted to want to trust Him, to love Him.

I am still working on that, honestly.

The day I saw my little girl's heartbeat on a monitor for the first time, something changed in me. I didn't mind ruining my own life, but I didn't want to ruin the life of my daughter.

I named her Hope.

And just as I choose to wake up and care for my daughter each day, I choose to follow the God I don't always understand.

I brought Hope back to Haiti with me when I went back to take care of the property. It was good to face the land, the community, and the life there. I dug trenches on the land where our house once stood. As I dug up the dirt, I found items that were once in our home.

I filled the trenches with new dirt and planted trees, hoping good fruit might grow in this place that represented both beautiful and painful memories. And it was good. I felt like I could move forward after that, although I still feel as if I will never be completely healed.

Poet Amanda Lovelace describes so much of what I feel:

"Where do all the memories go, the ones we hide away with lock and key yet continue to shape us all the same?"

"... I let myself know that my life doesn't have to be over just because theirs are and i went ahead and painted the sun back into my sky."

Katrina and I have long talks about life after trauma. And she is right that life never really gets back to the way it was before a traumatic loss, but it *can* be good again.

We can, in time, paint the sun back into our skies.

While healing is possible, no one can be expected to simply "get over it." The same is true of abuse. Informing ourselves and others about abuse and learning the ways of predators helps us become more aware of the dangers around us. These are things we need to know because of just how imperfect it is here.

For me, the journey toward healing involved both unlearning and learning. It involved giving myself permission to process my feelings honestly and create spaces for others to do the same. I learned how to receive help from others and how to be vulnerable. Vulnerability allows us to grapple with questions we might not otherwise ask, and results in seeing life and faith in new ways. We are forced to become more honest when all our former coping mechanisms don't serve us anymore. These are the moments when we begin to arm ourselves with what we need to carry on with the rest of our lives.

I began by getting honest with God and myself. Much later, I became honest with others and, in doing so, invited the light of God's presence to illuminate my next steps. I learned to identify the lies I believed about myself that nearly sabotaged my story for good.

As a result, my eyes and ears are wide open to the pain of others now. I have become passionate about creating safe spaces where abuse is not tolerated, and survivors feel safe enough to tell the truth. Like my brother, Chub, I now know how to throw a lifeline to others when they need it. Maybe it's a phone call, and if someone says they're fine, maybe it's asking a second time.

I also learned, through Jonas's forgiveness, to offer forgiveness and grace to the broken people I love. I once thought I could never forgive Pastor—"the beast" as my sisters and I often called him—yet I had to extend forgiveness for my sake, not his.

I had a reporter ask me one time, "Have you forgiven your perpetrator?"

I remember pausing, then I looked at her and said, "Come to think of it, I have never lost anything by forgiving someone who hurt me. But I nearly lost my life by not forgiving."

It took a long time, but now I understand that the same grace I have received is available to everyone—even him.

———•◦•———

I often say that I am here today because of Jesus and Jonas. So, I can't think of a better way to wrap up this picture of imperfection than for you hear from the two of them.

Jesus says, "Come to me, all of you who are weary and carry heavy burdens, and I will give you rest. Take my yoke upon you. Let me teach you, because I am humble and gentle at heart, and you will find rest for your souls." (Matthew 11:27-29 NLT)

He longs for us to lay down the heavy things we've been lugging around in solitude. He wants to enter our pain with us, so we don't have to walk alone. Every hurt we've felt, He also felt. Jonas expresses so beautifully his own perspective of our imperfect, painful journey here.

> *This kind of story takes something from people you can't put back. My wife has been stolen from. I see the tracks that have been left on the souls of her and our daughters every day. When I see all these kinds of stories coming out on the news, I wonder, "Where are all the men?"*
>
> *The worst day of my life was the day Anne told me what had been going on for six years.*
>
> *I can tell you, as a husband and a father, that wiped me out. When I received this information about my wife, I knew my family was broken and had to heal, but I had no idea how to do that. The part of my journey that felt unfair was that I didn't*

do anything wrong. But the spotlight was on me to see how I was going to handle this.

Why was I the one on the hot seat?

Most men don't know what to do. You go back and forth between "Why did it happen?" and "Why did you let it happen?"

I have watched my wife and two daughters go through that. There aren't many things that take a whack at your soul like that does. When guys hear their wives or daughters have been so deeply hurt by other men, I believe most of them don't want to go there. It's too complicated; they don't know what to do. I didn't know how to rise above the guilt that came from not being able to protect my own wife and my own kids. These devils are right under our feet. They are everywhere in our society ... sometimes even in our own homes.

I was always taught that "Just dogs get mad" and "Anger is of the devil." So, I learned to stuff it for a long time.

But I can remember feeling angry and wanting revenge. I knew I was justified. A small voice said, "Vengeance is mine."

I would often get together with my two brothers-in-law and a friend and we would talk about ways to even the score. But ultimately, we decided we were more committed to saving our families than making him pay for what he did. The last thing our wives needed was to be traumatized all over again. But being able to talk about what we would do if we could helped us hang on some days.

It's common for husbands to give up because we don't feel equipped to help. Because of my culture and upbringing, I was taught, "You never quit when you're family."

That's what made me fight so hard for my family.

Healing looks different to everyone. You have to get new information, outside of what you already know, to move ahead. Your history doesn't change, but your interpretation changes over time. You can't edit events out of your history, but you can see those things in a new light. That's healing.

I felt stripped of my masculinity, spirituality, and self-esteem. Today, I don't feel like I did then. That's healing.

The lie that I've heard all my life is "Forgive and forget." But the mind forgets nothing. We're going to remember. We have to manage that instead of letting it manage us. That's healing.

If you want to heal it, you have to feel it. Telling your story is healing and helps bring together the memories stored in your brain with your conscious mind. It helps you make peace with your past. You will keep remembering new details and you'll keep putting them where they need to be by telling your story.

People say, "If you forgive you'll feel better."

I'm not sure about that.

There is no timeline for healing and forgiveness. You can't force those things. When a counselor asks how we feel, most of us aren't going to share how we actually feel but try to answer the way we are "supposed" to feel. We don't realize that the way we feel is the right way. God wants us to be free. He doesn't put us on a timeline for that freedom. I used to scold myself if I had a bad day, if I had thoughts of anger or revenge. But God understands.

You're GOING to have bad days. Bad days don't mean you aren't healing. You're normal. Who said you have to have a good day every day? Why do we think we aren't going to have bad days?

Grace, hard work, change, new information ... so much has taken place in our life since 1982. When I have a bad day, I'm not going backwards. I'm still moving forward. I know more now than I did then.

When I think about Angie, hours of data are loaded into my brain. Just one thought of Angie brings that data to the forefront and so many memories and emotions come up. There was a time when those emotions would overwhelm me for days. Now, I might be able to function again within an hour or so. That's healing.

I believe in the hope of Heaven. And I can hardly wait to see Angie. When I do, all the days I will get with her there will more than make up for those I have missed with her here.

You get tired of this world at times.

But this is not the last chapter.

Even at its very best, life here in this world is imperfect. People are broken. WE are broken. All we can do is cling to what is true, surround ourselves with people who are willing to walk with us, and look forward to what is next.

CONCLUSION

Is That Too Much for You?

When our grandson, Ryan, was only four years old, there was one day he was riding around our property on a four-wheeler while I picked up twigs. Before long, I was carrying more sticks than I could realistically hold, without even realizing how large my load had become.

Ryan rode up to me, and in his sweet, innocent way said, "NeeNee, is that too much for you?"

I looked at my load, then I looked at him, realizing how full my arms had become—one stick at a time.

Then he added, "If you want, I can help you with that!"

Inviting one another to share our stories and pain is as simple as that. It is about sharing the weight of it all—instead of trying to carry it alone—with someone who wants to help.

Ryan's words are the words I want to leave you with.

When the burdens and secrets we carry begin to stack up, imagine living in a world where we can say to one another, "Is that too much for you? If you want, I can help you with that."

Endnotes

1   Smith, S. G., Chen, J., Basile, K. C., Gilbert, L. K., Merrick, M. T., Patel, N., ... Jain, A. (2017). The National Intimate Partner and Sexual Violence Survey (NISVS): 2010-2012 state report. Retrieved from the Centers for Disease Control and Prevention, National Center for Injury Prevention and Control: https://www.cdc.gov/violenceprevention/pdf/NISVS-StateReportBook.pdf

2   "Domestic Violence Against Women: Recognize Patterns, Seek Help." *Mayo Clinic*. Mayo Clinic Health System, March 1, 2017. Web. January 18, 2018.

3   "When Wolves Wear Shepherds' Clothing: Helping Women Survive Clergy Sexual Abuse." Diane Garland. 2006. *Journal of the North American Association of Christians in Social Work.*

4   Smith, S. G., Chen, J., Basile, K. C., Gilbert, L. K., Merrick, M. T., Patel, N., ... Jain, A. (2017). The National Intimate Partner and Sexual Violence Survey (NISVS): 2010-2012 state report. Retrieved from the Centers for Disease Control and Prevention, National Center for Injury Prevention and Control: https://www.cdc.gov/violenceprevention/pdf/NISVS-StateReportBook.pdf

5   Brennan Manning, "The Ragamuffin Gospel: Good News for the Bedraggled, Beat-Up, and Burt Out" (Multnomah Books, 2005)

Acknowledgements

Over my lifetime, I wouldn't have experienced the level of success and satisfaction I did if it wasn't for the support of others, books I've read, and inspiring people I've encountered. Thank you to all of those who have cheered me on and encouraged me in my journey. It was the things you said and the new information you shared that gave me the courage to keep going. Most of the time, I was out of my league, and your support and dedication carried me through.

To those who helped make this book possible, I'm forever grateful. Thank you.

To my husband—I'm here because of you. Your grace, the Jesus-Love you model, and the never critical approach you take with me are the reasons we are happily married and experienced our 50th anniversary. You made me feel safe when I didn't feel safe being alone. Your patience with me has astounded me. The best choice I ever made was marrying you and I still feel like the luckiest girl in the world. I love you.

To Emily—I'm so glad you entered my life at the right time and the right place. I felt connected with you heart-to-heart. There were so many common threads that knit us together even before

I knew your story. The things we had in common really gave me the assurance that you understood my story and would write it in the beautiful, impactful way you did.

To Gentry—Without you, I truly would not be writing another book. You are the one who came to me at a time when I thought God was finished with me. I had given up on my dreams and passions. My head said I was done, but my heart knew I wasn't. When you came into the picture again, there was something that ignited in my spirit, and I knew I was beginning something new.

To my sisters, Becky and Fi—We've always done everything together. The good and the bad. We went to hell and back ... together. Our stories are connected in a very deep, spiritual way that I can't describe. Thanks for being willing to share your lives with every reader. I am so proud of you. I feel incredibly honored that you would do this. It's amazing to me that we're still here and still together. I love you both dearly.

To all the courageous individuals who shared their stories in this book—Fi, Becky, LaWonna, Kate, Kim, Gretchen, Katrina, Sue, Emily, and Todd—Thank you for your willingness to share your deep pain in a public way. I understand how difficult that is. You could have said no, but you said yes. Even though these stories are abbreviated versions of your life, you have shared the most vulnerable. Every person that is vulnerable in the written form is courageous and strong. Thank you for being brave. I am deeply grateful, and you inspire me.

To my daughters, LaWonna and LaVale—I know you have been through a lot with me. The death of Angela impacted my motherhood and changed the trajectory of our entire family. I'm grateful for your unending patience with me. You felt the abandonment of a mother in deep grief and pain and yet through the years we've been able to work through our issues in ways that were meaningful.

I know we're not done yet. The abuse we experienced as a family put us into deep trauma and I didn't understand its impact for many years. We have struggled through all of it because we believe in family. Thank you for expressing your love and forgiveness to me. I'm proud of you both and I love you more than I can express.

To my mom and daddy who are now in heaven looking down—I know you have watched me all these years. I feel your presence. Thank you for the heritage that you left for me rooted in God, faith, and family. I look forward to one day seeing you to say thank you with a full understanding of what that now means.

To all my siblings—you may not know how much you have truly inspired me my entire life. From early memories, to today, just being a part of your lives has enriched mine. Thank you for being the best brothers and sisters that I could ever have.

To Mark Means—My newfound friend who is the most genuine, real, caring, helpful, and dear person. Thank you for your input in these pages, your inspiration, and giving me insights about trauma. You have taught me that everyone has a story and everyone I meet has pain. Thank you for opening me up to see this truth all around me.

To all the musicians and artists for your music that lifted me out of the depths of my despair, encouraged me, and gave me the will to live. When nothing else made sense and I was all alone, your songs would penetrate my heart.

To our editor, Aubrey—thank you for taking our words and making them even better! Your touches throughout the book have helped turn it into something greater.

To the team at Morgan James Publishing—Thank you for believing in these stories and accepting them to the point that you would publish them. It's humbling and encouraging that you thought it was worthy of such an honor.

Next Steps

Are you interested in bringing Anne's inspirational story and message to your event?

Anne is a dynamic and inspirational speaker, sharing from her own experience, about the power of purpose and overcoming pain, blame, and shame to live a life of freedom. Her unique experience of building a successful business while fighting despair, defeat, and depression gives her a unique story that resonates with business and faith-based audiences alike. She is a favorite among leadership events, universities, churches, and women's conferences.

To learn more about upcoming events, initiatives and to inquire about booking Anne, please visit us at www.auntieannebeiler.com or contact us via email at hello@auntieannebeiler.com.

About the Authors

AUNTIE ANNE BEILER

Anne Beiler began twisting pretzels in 1987 to support her husband's vision of offering free counseling services in their community. What began as a single farmer's market stand grew into Auntie Anne's Inc., the world's largest hand rolled soft pretzel franchise.

Anne's journey towards success began many years before the first pretzel was rolled when she and her husband experienced any parent's worst nightmare: the loss of a child. This propelled Anne into years of darkness, depression, and despair but out of her pain came purpose and the desire to persevere towards personal and professional success.

Anne is among an elite group of women who have founded national companies in America and is one of an even smaller number who have owned an international franchise company. She was named one of America's 500 Women Entrepreneurs by Working Women and Entrepreneur of the Year by Inc. Magazine. Anne's Entrepreneurial insights and personal story have been featured on many television shows including Secret Millionaire, The Oprah Winfrey Show, Good Morning America, ANDERSON, and Food Court Wars. Her story has been highlighted in numerous publications including Fortune Magazine, Inc Magazine, Guidepost, and Nation's Restaurant News. Anne also received honorary doctorates from Eastern College and Elizabethtown College.

Anne sold Auntie Anne's in 2005 and authored *Twist of Faith*, a revealing look at the inner workings of her life while building an international corporation. Today, she speaks to audiences around the world, inspiring people with her authentic stories and message of overcoming. She is on a mission to help women find their voice and break free from the secrets that keep them stuck in pain, blame, and shame.

Anne and her husband live in Texas and are parents to two daughters, both married, and proud grandparents to four grandchildren.

Find Anne online at www.auntieannebeiler.com and on social networks at instagram.com/auntieanneb and facebook.com/auntieannebeiler.

EMILY SUTHERLAND

Emily Sutherland is an internationally recognized storyteller whose body of work spans a broad spectrum of genres and mediums, ranging from television and radio, to books and magazines, to podcasts and the blogosphere.

Her unique specialty is finding the heart, soul, and voice inside every subject with a blend of raw authenticity and genuine compassion. She has lent her voice to countless biographical stories, essays, and articles on the subjects of creativity, philanthropy, spirituality, relationships, leadership, hospitality, and personal growth.

With more than twenty years of professional experience in the music industry, her name appears in the credits of dozens of Billboard chart-topping volumes produced by Gaither Television Productions, which air on television networks around the world. Her multifaceted roles as an executive staff member provided opportunities to excel in a variety of disciplines, including mass communication, ghostwriting, photo journalism, artist management, video production, web content creation, personal and professional blogging, public relations, and general market product launches.

As an editorial board member for the entire 15-year life of Gaither Music's niche publication, she contributed cover features, columns, artist interviews and photo journalistic stories.

The children's book she released in 2017, *It's Hard To Hug a Porcupine*, tells a timely story of the healing power of kindness toward people who are difficult to love.

Emily and her husband, Scott, are cofounders of the Love Better movement (www.lovebetter.world) and hosts of The Love Better Podcasts.

Printed in the USA
CPSIA information can be obtained
at www.ICGtesting.com
JSHW022340140824
68134JS00019B/1596